Getting Haiti Right
This Time

The U.S. and the Coup

Noam Chomsky
Paul Farmer
Amy Goodman

Common Courage Press   Monroe, Maine

Copyright © 2004 by Noam Chomsky, Paul Farmer,
    Amy Goodman
All rights reserved.
Cover design by Matt Wuerker
Cover photos by Panos Pictures

ISBN 1-56751-318-2 paper
ISBN 1-56751-319-0 cloth

**Library of Congress Cataloging-in-Publication Data is
available on request from the publisher**

Common Courage Press
121 Red Barn Road
Monroe, ME 04951
800-497-3207

FAX (207) 525-3068
orders-info@commoncouragepress.com

See our website for e versions of this book.
www.commoncouragepress.com

Printed in Canada
First Printing

The title comes from a phrase by Ambassador James Dobbins, Special Envoy to Haiti under President Clinton, 1994-96, and President Bush's Special Envoy to Afghanistan following the 911 attacks, talking to National Public Radio the morning after the coup, February 29, 2004:

> "All too likely this cycle will be repeated in the future unless we get it right this time."

Spoken in the Washington dialect:

> President Aristide had "worn out his welcome."
> —Vice President Dick Cheney, whose own
> administration was hand-picked by the U.S.
> Supreme Court, an institution that is, in
> turn, controlled by Republican appointees.

Translation:

> One good coup deserves another.

Contents

Democracy Now! Interviews

CHAPTER ONE

The "Noble Phase" and "Saintly Glow" of US Foreign Policy

Noam Chomsky

March 9, 2004

Those who have any concern for Haiti will naturally want to understand how its most recent tragedy has been unfolding. And for those who have had the privilege of any contact with the people of this tortured land, it is not just natural but inescapable. Nevertheless, we make a serious error if we focus too narrowly on the events of the recent past, or even on Haiti alone. The crucial issue for us is what we should be doing about what is taking place. That would be true even if our options and our responsibility were limited; far more so when they are immense and decisive, as in the case of Haiti. And even more so because the course of the terrible story was predictable years ago—if we failed to act to prevent it. And fail we did. The lessons are clear, and so important that they would be the topic of daily front-page articles in a free press.

Reviewing what was taking place in Haiti shortly after Clinton "restored democracy" in 1994, I was compelled to conclude, unhappily, in Z Magazine that "It would not be very surprising, then, if the Haitian operations become another catastrophe," and if so, "It is not a difficult chore to trot out the familiar phrases that will explain the failure of our mission of benevolence in this failed society." The reasons were evident to anyone who chose to look. And the familiar phrases again resound, sadly and predictably.

There is much solemn discussion today explaining, correctly, that democracy means more than flipping a lever every few years. Functioning democracy has preconditions. One is that the population should have some way to learn what is happening in the world. The real world, not the self-serving portrait offered by the "establishment press," which is disfigured by its "subservience to state power" and "the usual hostility to popular movements"—the accurate words of Paul Farmer, whose work on Haiti is, in its own way, perhaps even as remarkable as what he has accomplished within the country. Farmer was writing in 1993, reviewing mainstream commentary and reporting on Haiti, a disgraceful record that goes back to the days of Wilson's vicious and destructive invasion in 1915, and on to the present. The facts are extensively documented, appalling, and shameful. And they are deemed irrelevant for the usual reasons: they do not conform to the required self-image, and so are efficiently dispatched deep into the memory hole, though they can be unearthed by those who have some interest in the real world.

They will rarely be found, however, in the "establishment press." Keeping to the more liberal and knowledgeable end of the spectrum, the standard version is that in "failed states" like Haiti and Iraq the US must become engaged in benevolent "nation-building" to "enhance democracy," a "noble goal" but one that may be beyond our means because of the inadequacies of the objects of our solicitude. In Haiti, despite Washington's dedicated efforts from Wilson to FDR while the country was under Marine occupation, "the new dawn of Haitian democracy never came." And "not all America's good wishes, nor all its Marines, can achieve [democracy today] until the Haitians do it themselves" (H.D.S. Greenway, *Boston Globe*). As *New York Times* correspondent R.W. Apple recounted two centuries of history in 1994, reflecting on the prospects for Clinton's endeavor to "restore democracy" then underway, "Like the

French in the 19th century, like the Marines who occupied Haiti from 1915 to 1934, the American forces who are trying to impose a new order will confront a complex and violent society with no history of democracy."

Apple does appear to go a bit beyond the norm in his reference to Napoleon's savage assault on Haiti, leaving it in ruins, in order to prevent the crime of liberation in the world's richest colony, the source of much of France's wealth. But perhaps that undertaking too satisfies the fundamental criterion of benevolence: it was supported by the United States, which was naturally outraged and frightened by "the first nation in the world to argue the case of universal freedom for all humankind, revealing the limited definition of freedom adopted by the French and American revolutions." So Haitian historian Patrick Bellegarde-Smith writes, accurately describing the terror in the slave state next door, which was not relieved even when Haiti's successful liberation struggle, at enormous cost, opened the way to the expansion to the West by compelling Napoleon to accept the Louisiana Purchase. The US continued to do what it could to strangle Haiti, even supporting France's insistence that Haiti pay a huge indemnity for the crime of liberating itself, a burden it has never escaped—and France, of course, dismisses with elegant disdain Haiti's request, recently under Aristide, that it at least repay the indemnity, forgetting the responsibilities that a civilized society would accept.

The basic contours of what led to the current tragedy are pretty clear. Just beginning with the 1990 election of Aristide (far too narrow a time frame), Washington was appalled by the election of a populist candidate with a grass-roots constituency just as it had been appalled by the prospect of the hemisphere's first free country on its doorstep two centuries earlier. Washington's traditional allies in Haiti naturally agreed. "The fear of democracy exists, by definitional necessity, in elite groups who monopolize economic and political power," Bellegarde-Smith observes in his perceptive history of Haiti

(*Haiti: The Breached Citadel*); whether in Haiti or the US or anywhere else.

The threat of democracy in Haiti in 1991 was even more ominous because of the favorable reaction of the international financial institutions (World Bank, Inter-American Development Bank) to Aristide's programs, which awakened traditional concerns over the "virus" effect of successful independent development. These are familiar themes in international affairs: American independence aroused similar concerns among European leaders. The dangers are commonly perceived to be particularly grave in a country like Haiti, which had been ravaged by France and then reduced to utter misery by a century of US intervention. If even people in such dire circumstances can take their fate into their own hands, who knows what might happen elsewhere as the "contagion spreads."

The Bush I administration reacted to the disaster of democracy by shifting aid from the democratically elected government to what are called "democratic forces": the wealthy elites and the business sectors, who, along with the murderers and torturers of the military and paramilitaries, had been lauded by the current incumbents in Washington, in their Reaganite phase, for their progress in "democratic development," justifying lavish new aid. The praise came in response to ratification by the Haitian people of a law granting Washington's client killer and torturer Baby Doc Duvalier the authority to suspend the rights of any political party without reasons. The referendum passed by a majority of 99.98%. It therefore marked a positive step towards democracy as compared with the 99% approval of a 1918 law granting US corporations the right to turn the country into a US plantation, passed by 5% of the population after the Haitian Parliament was disbanded at gunpoint by Wilson's Marines when it refused to accept this "progressive measure," essential for "economic development." Their reaction to Baby Doc's encouraging progress towards democracy was characteristic—worldwide—

on the part of the visionaries who are now entrancing educated opinion with their dedication to bringing democracy to a suffering world—although, to be sure, their actual exploits are being tastefully rewritten to satisfy current needs.

Refugees fleeing to the US from the terror of the US-backed dictatorships were forcefully returned, in gross violation of international humanitarian law. The policy was reversed when a democratically elected government took office. Though the flow of refugees reduced to a trickle, they were mostly granted political asylum. Policy returned to normal when a military junta overthrew the Aristide government after seven months, and state terrorist atrocities rose to new heights. The perpetrators were the army—the inheritors of the National Guard left by Wilson's invaders to control the population—and its paramilitary forces. The most important of these, FRAPH, was founded by CIA asset Emmanuel Constant, who now lives happily in Queens, Clinton and Bush II having dismissed extradition requests—because he would reveal US ties to the murderous junta, it is widely assumed. Constant's contributions to state terror were, after all, meager; merely prime responsibility for the murder of 4-5000 poor blacks.

Recall the core element of the Bush doctrine, which has "already become a de facto rule of international relations," Harvard's Graham Allison writes in *Foreign Affairs*: "those who harbor terrorists are as guilty as the terrorists themselves," in the President's words, and must be treated accordingly, by large-scale bombing and invasion.

When Aristide was overthrown by the 1991 military coup, the Organization of American States declared an embargo. Bush I announced that the US would violate it by exempting US firms. He was thus "fine tuning" the embargo for the benefit of the suffering population, the *New York Times* reported. Clinton authorized even more extreme violations of the embargo: US trade with the junta and its wealthy supporters sharply increased. The crucial element of the embargo was, of course, oil. While the CIA solemnly testified to Congress that the junta "probably will be out of fuel and power very shortly" and "Our intelligence efforts are focused on detecting attempts to circumvent the embargo and monitoring its impact," Clinton secretly authorized the Texaco Oil Company to ship oil to the junta illegally, in violation of presidential directives. This remarkable revelation was the lead story on the AP wires the day before Clinton sent the Marines to "restore democracy," impossible to miss—I happened to be monitoring AP wires that day and saw it repeated prominently over and over—and obviously of enormous significance for anyone who wanted to understand what was happening. It was suppressed with truly impressive discipline, though reported in industry journals along with scant mention buried in the business press.

Also efficiently suppressed were the crucial conditions that Clinton imposed for Aristide's return: that he adopt the program of the defeated U.S.-backed candidate in the 1990 elections, a former World Bank official who had received 14% of the vote. We call this "restoring democracy," a prime illustration of how US foreign policy has entered a "noble phase" with a "saintly glow," the national press explained. The harsh neoliberal program that Aristide was compelled to adopt was virtually guaranteed to demolish the remaining shreds of economic sovereignty, extending Wilson's progressive legislation and similar US-imposed measures since.

As democracy was thereby restored, the World Bank announced that "The renovated state must focus on an economic strategy centered on the energy and initiative of Civil Society, especially the private sector, both national and foreign." That has the merit of honesty: Haitian Civil Society includes the tiny rich elite and US corporations, but not the vast majority of the population, the peasants and slum-dwellers who had committed the grave sin of organizing to elect their own president. World Bank officers explained that the neoliberal program would benefit the "more open, enlightened, business class" and foreign investors, but assured us that the program "is not going to hurt the poor to the extent it has in other countries" subjected to structural adjustment, because the Haitian poor already lacked minimal protection from proper economic policy, such as subsidies for basic goods. Aristide's minister in charge of rural development and agrarian reform was not notified of the plans to be imposed on this largely peasant society, to be returned by "America's good wishes" to the track from which it veered briefly after the regrettable democratic election in 1990.

Matters then proceeded in their predictable course. A 1995 USAID report explained that the "export-driven trade and investment policy" that Washington imposed will "relentlessly squeeze the domestic rice farmer," who will be forced to turn to agroexport, with incidental benefits to US agribusiness and investors. Despite their extreme poverty, Haitian rice farmers are quite efficient, but cannot possibly compete with US agribusiness, even if it did not receive 40% of its profits from government subsidies, sharply increased under the Reaganites who are again in power, still producing enlightened rhetoric about the miracles of the market. We now read that Haiti cannot feed itself, another sign of a "failed state."

A few small industries were still able to function, for example, making chicken parts. But US conglomerates have a large surplus of dark meat, and therefore demanded the right to dump their excess products in Haiti. They tried to do the same in Canada and Mexico too, but there illegal dumping could be barred. Not in Haiti, compelled to submit to efficient market principles by the US government and the corporations it serves.

One might note that the Pentagon's proconsul in Iraq, Paul Bremer, ordered a very similar program to be instituted there, with the same beneficiaries in mind. That's also called "enhancing democracy." In fact, the record, highly revealing and important, goes back to the 18th century. Similar programs had a large role in creating today's third world. Meanwhile the powerful ignored the rules, except when they could benefit from them, and were able to become rich developed societies; dramatically the US, which led the way in modern protectionism and, particularly since World War II, has relied crucially on the dynamic state sector for innovation and development, socializing risk and cost.

The punishment of Haiti became much more severe under Bush II—there are differences within the narrow spectrum of cruelty and greed. Aid was cut and international institutions were pressured to do likewise, under pretexts too outlandish to merit discussion. They are extensively reviewed in Paul Farmer's *Uses of Haiti*, and in some current press commentary, notably by Jeffrey Sachs (*Financial Times*) and Tracy Kidder (*New York Times*).

Putting details aside, what has happened since is eerily similar to the overthrow of Haiti's first democratic government in 1991. The Aristide government, once again, was undermined by US planners, who understood, under Clinton, that the threat of democracy can be overcome if economic sovereignty is eliminated, and presumably also understood that economic development will also be a faint hope under such conditions, one of the best-confirmed lessons of economic history. Bush II planners are even more dedicated to undermining democracy and independence, and despised Aristide and the popular organizations that swept him to power with perhaps even more passion than their predecessors. The forces that reconquered the country are mostly inheritors of the US-installed army and paramilitary terrorists.

Those who are intent on diverting attention from the US role will object that the situation is more complex—as is always true—and that Aristide too was guilty of many crimes. Correct, but if he had been a saint the situation would hardly have developed very differently, as was evident in 1994, when the only real hope was that a democratic revolution in the US would make it possible to shift policy in a more civilized direction.

What is happening now is awful, maybe beyond repair. And there is plenty of short-term responsibility on all sides. But the right way for the US and France to proceed is very clear. They should begin with payment of enormous reparations to Haiti (France is perhaps even more hypocritical and disgraceful in this regard than the US). That, however, requires construction of functioning democratic societies in which, at the very least, people have a prayer of knowing what's going on. Commentary on Haiti, Iraq, and other "failed societies" is quite right in stressing the importance of overcoming the "democratic deficit" that substantially reduces the significance of elections. It does not, however, draw the obvious corollary: the lesson applies in spades to a country where "politics is the shadow cast on society by big business," in the words of America's leading social philosopher, John Dewey, describing his own country in days when the blight had spread nowhere near as far as it has today.

For those who are concerned with the substance of democracy and human rights, the basic tasks at home are also clear enough. They have been carried out before, with no slight success, and under incomparably harsher conditions elsewhere, including the slums and hills of Haiti. We do not have to submit, voluntarily, to living in a failed state suffering from an enormous democratic deficit.

CHAPTER TWO

> "I declare in overthrowing me they have uprooted the trunk of the tree of peace, but it will grow back because the roots are Louverturian,"
> —Jean Bertrand Aristide

What Happened in Haiti?

Where Past is Present

Paul Farmer

March 12, 2004

On the night of February 28, 2004, Haitian president Jean-Bertrand Aristide was forced from power, in part by an armed uprising of former members of the military, disbanded in 1995. Aristide claimed he was kidnapped and did not know where he was being taken until the very end of a 20-hour flight, when he was informed that he and his wife would be landing "in a French military base in the middle of Africa." He found himself in the Central African Republic.

Whenever Haiti does intrude into America's consciousness, people like me—old Haiti hands who have lived and worked here and written about the place over the years—are consulted on "the current crisis." The current crisis isn't something that started in January 2004: it has been going on for the past couple of decades and longer. I've found, however, that if you try to discuss the roots of the problem, journalists and policymakers are likely to cut you off, saying: "Let's not dwell on the past. What should be done about Haiti's future?"

Nonetheless, a quick review of Haiti's history is indispensable to understanding the current muddle. We begin in the eighteenth century, when a slave colony on Haiti, then called Santo Domingo, became France's most valuable colonial possession. According to historians, Santo Domingo stands out as perhaps the most brutal slave colony in human history. It was the leading port of call for slave ships during the latter half of the eighteenth century, and a third of new arrivals died within a few years of reaching the colony. On the eve of the French Revolution, the bit of real estate now dismissed as a failed state was producing two-thirds of Europe's tropical produce. Many of France's beautiful coastal cities, including Bordeaux, are monuments to the slave trade. These facts are already forgotten outside Haiti.

Haitians remember: they consider themselves living legacies of the slave trade and the bloody revolt, starting in 1791, that finally removed the French. Over a decade of war followed, during which France's largest expeditionary force was sent to quell the rebellion. As the French containment operation flagged, the Haitian slave general Toussaint Louverture, victorious in battle, was invited to a parley. No parley ensued: Toussaint was kidnapped and taken away to a prison in the mountains of France; he died there of exposure and tuberculosis. Every Haitian schoolchild knows by heart his last words: "In overthrowing me, you have cut down in San Domingo only the trunk of the tree of black liberty. It will spring up again by the roots for they are numerous and deep." Among those whose imaginations were fired by these events was William Wordsworth, who addressed Toussaint:

> Though fallen thyself, never to rise again,
> Live, and take comfort. Thou hast left behind
> Powers that will work for thee; air, earth, and skies;
> There's not a breathing of the common wind
> That will forget thee; thou hast great allies;
> Thy friends are exultations, agonies,
> And love, and man's unconquerable mind.

Wordsworth was wrong about allies. The slaves in revolt had few friends, and the war continued in Haiti, with Europe's chief colonial powers—France, England and Spain—caught up in the fray. In November 1803, the former slaves won what proved to be the war's final battle and on January 1, 1804 declared the independent republic of Haiti. It was Latin America's first independent country and the only nation ever born of a slave revolt. Virtually all of the world's powers sided with France against the self-proclaimed Black Republic, which declared itself a haven not only for all runaway slaves but also for indigenous people (the true natives of Haiti had succumbed to infectious disease and Spanish slavery well before the arrival of the French). Hemmed in by slave colonies, Haiti had only one non-colonized neighbor, the slaveholding United States, which refused to recognize Haiti's independence. As one US senator from South Carolina put it, speaking from the Senate floor in 1824, "Our policy with regard to Hayti [sic] is plain. We never can acknowledge her independence.... The peace and safety of a large portion of our union forbids us even to discuss it."

Haiti's leaders were desperate for recognition, since the only goods the island had to sell were sugar, coffee, cotton, and other tropical produce. In 1825, under threat of another French invasion and the restoration of slavery, Haitian officials signed what was to prove the beginning of the end of any hope of autonomy: King Charles X agreed to recognize Haiti's independence only if the new republic paid an indemnity of 150 million francs and consented to the reduction of import and export taxes for French goods.

It may be impossible to put a price on the toll taken by slavery—the destruction not only of lives and families, but of cultures and languages—but the same cannot be said about "the French debt." One hundred fifty million gold francs amounts to about half a billion US dollars in the most conservative estimate, without attempting to calculate 175 years of interest and inflation. Unusually, reintroducing slavery was not legal at the time, even under French law. The "debt" that Haiti recognized was incurred by the slaves' having deprived the French owners not only of land and equipment but of their human "property." The threat of force made it more akin to extortion than compensation.

By any account, the impact of the debt repayments— which continued until after World War II—was devastating. Assessments by Haitians are severe: anthropologist Jean Price-Mars, referring to the Haitian leaders who yielded to French threats, complained in 1953 that their "incompetence and frivolity... made a country whose revenues and outflows had been balanced up to then into a nation burdened with debt and trapped in financial obligations that could never be satisfied." French abolitionist Victor Schoelcher argued that "imposing an indemnity on the victorious slaves was equivalent to making them pay with money that which they had already paid with their blood." Even those who profited from the deal knew that Haiti's economy was being dealt a lethal blow.

When capital moves up a steep grade of inequality—from a war-devastated colony of former slaves to one of the world's most powerful nations—the greater happiness of the greatest number is not being served; rather, those who have little to spare are forced to give up essentials so that others can add to their luxuries. Such transfers from the poor to the rich continue to this day, with some of the international financial institutions serving as cheerleaders for analogous—albeit more subtly practiced—processes.

In the late nineteenth century, the United States eclipsed France as a prevailing force in Haitian affairs. A US military occupation (1915-1934) brought back *corvée* labor and introduced aerial bombing, two symptoms of the vast disparity in power between occupier and occupied. Officials sitting at desks in Washington, D.C. created institutions that Haitians would have to live with. For example, the Haitian army that today claims to have the country "in its hands" and seeks to be reestablished was created not by Haitians but by an act of the U.S. Congress. From its founding during the US occupation until it was demobilized by Aristide in 1995, the Haitian army has never known a non-Haitian enemy. Internal enemies, however, it had aplenty.

This state of affairs—military-backed governments, dictatorships, chronic instability, repression, the heavy hand of Washington over all—continued throughout the 20th century. When I first traveled to Haiti in 1983, the Duvalier family dictatorship had been in place for a quarter of a century. There was no free press—and no dissent, to be sure, from radios or newspapers; no politicians declaring themselves the heads of parallel governments. The Duvaliers and their military dealt with all such threats ruthlessly, while the judiciary and the rest of the world looked the other way. Haiti was already the poorest country in the Western world, and those who ran it argued, with a certain sociological confidence, that force is required to police deep poverty.

By the mid-1980s, however, the hunger, despair, and disease that are the lot of most Haitians was beyond management, even by force. Baby Doc Duvalier, named "President for Life" at age 19, fled the country in 1986. A first attempt at democratic elections, in 1987, led to a massacre at the polling station. An army general declared himself in charge. In September 1988, the mayor of Port-au-Prince—himself a former military officer—paid a gang to burn down a downtown Roman Catholic church while it was packed with people attending mass. At the altar was none other than Father Jean-Bertrand Aristide, nemesis of the dictatorship and the army and a proponent of liberation theology. This stream of Catholic thought had been sweeping Latin America with its injunctions that the Church proclaim "a preferential option for the poor." It had its adversaries: Pope John Paul II, for one, and President Ronald Reagan. Members of Reagan's brain trust, participating in a 1980 meeting in Santa Fe, New Mexico, declared liberation theology less

Christian than Communist and recommended that "U.S. policy must begin to counter (not react against)... the 'liberation theology' clergy."

Aristide's rise from slum priest to presidential candidate took place against a backdrop of right-wing death squad activity and threatened military coups. He rose quickly in the eyes of the Haitians, but his stock plummeted with the United States and its press. The *New York Times*, which relies heavily on informants who speak English or French instead of only Haitian Creole, had few kind words for the priest: "Among the business community, pessimistic reactions run stronger," ran a news story published three days prior to Haiti's first elections. "'He is a cross between Ayatollah and Fidel,' one downtown businessman said in a typical assessment of Father Aristide from those in the entrepreneurial class. 'If it comes to a choice between the ultra-left and the ultra-right, I am ready to form an alliance with the ultra-right.'" Such coverage gave the impression that it might be a tight race. But Haitians knew that Aristide would easily win any democratic election, and on December 16, 1990, the priest won 67% of the popularvote in a field of 12 candidates.

The United States might not have been able to prevent Aristide's landslide victory, but there was much they could do to undermine him. The most effective method, adopted by the first Bush administration, was to fund the opposition—its poor showing at the polls was no reason, it appears, to cut off aid to them—and the military. Declassified records now make it clear that the CIA and other US organizations helped to create and fund a paramilitary group called FRAPH, which rose to prominence after the September 1991 military coup that ousted Aristide. Thousands of civilians were killed outright and hundred of thousands fled onto the high seas and across the border to the Dominican Republic.

Whether it was the refugee question or a change of heart in foreign policy—Bill Clinton mentioned the Haitian refugees in many of his campaign speeches—Aristide became, in

October 1994, the first exiled Latin American president to return to office, with a little over a year left in his term. Although the 1994 US military intervention was authorized by the United Nations and indisputably stopped bloodshed and restored constitutional rule, other forces were at play: the restoration of Aristide was basically a United States show. Then, seven weeks after Aristide's return, Republicans took control of the US Congress. From that day forth, influential Republicans worked to block or burden with conditions aid to impoverished, strife-torn Haiti.

The aid through official channels was never very substantial. Counted per capita, the US was giving Haiti one-tenth what it was distributing in Kosovo. Claims heard recently from the mouths of former ambassadors and the second Bush administration—that hundreds of millions of dollars flowed to Haiti—are correct, though misleading. Aid did flow, just not to the elected government. A great deal of it went to non-governmental organizations and to the anti-Aristide opposition. A lot went to pay for the UN occupation and Halliburton support services. US organizations like the International Republican Institute and even the US Agency for International Development funneled hundreds of thousands, perhaps millions, of dollars to the opposition. The cuts in bilateral aid and the diversion of monies to the opposition meant there could be, in a country as poor as Haiti, little effort to build schools, health care infrastructure, roads, ports, telecommunications, or airports.

When the anti-Aristide opposition cried foul over a handful of contested parliamentary seats in the 2000 election, the US quickly acted to freeze international aid as well. Take, for example the case of the Inter-American Development Bank (IDB) loans. These loans—one for health care, another for education, one for potable water, and one for road improvement: areas of greatest need in Haiti, the timeliness of which would seem obvious to anyone—had been approved by the Haitian government and by the Bank's board of directors. The loans were then delayed for "political reasons." Haiti held local and parliamentary elections in May 2000, and eight parliamentary seats—out of approximately 7,500 posts filled that day—were disputed, even though all went to those with the greatest number of votes (those unhappy with the results demanded a run-off). Sources both Haitian and American confirmed to me that it was the United States that asked the Inter-American Development Bank to block the loans until these electoral disputes had been resolved. Since seven of the Senators in question resigned in 2001, and the other's term expired shortly thereafter, that should've been the end of the aid freeze. Instead, it continued throughout Aristide's tenure.

The IDB later claimed that this funding freeze occurred as the result of a consensus reached by the Organization of American States in something called "the Declaration of Quebec City." Interestingly enough, the Declaration is dated April 22, 2001, and the letter from the United States representative to the IDB asking that the loans not be disbursed was dated April 8, 2001. To quote the conclusion of one of the rare journalists to find this scandal worthy of inquiry, "it would seem that the effort became concerted after it was made."

International financial institutions have time and again engaged in discriminatory and probably illegal practices towards Haiti. According to the Haiti Support Group, "Haiti's debt to international financial institutions and foreign governments has grown from US$302 million in 1980 to US$1.134 billion today. About 40% of this debt stems from loans to the brutal Duvalier dictators who invested precious little of it in the country. This is known as 'odious debt' because it was used to oppress the people, and, according to international law, this debt need not be repaid." There has been relative silence in the press and among human rights groups on this score.

The story gets worse. In order to meet the renewed demands of the IDB, the cash-strapped Haitian Government was required to pay ever-expanding arrears, many of them linked to loans paid out to the Duvalier dictatorship and to the brutal military regimes of 1986-1990. In July 2003, Haiti sent over 90% of all its foreign reserves to Washington to pay these arrears. Yet as of today, less than US$4 million of the four blocked loans mentioned above has flowed to Haiti in spite of many assurances to the contrary from the IDB.

This startling echo of illegal practices in the nineteenth century—for the IDB payments will strike both lawyers and the Haitian poor as reminiscent of France's indemnity shakedown—is of a piece with many other discriminatory practices towards Haiti and its people. You'd think this might be newsworthy: the world's most powerful nations joining forces to block aid and humanitarian assistance to one of the poorest. But for three years this story was almost impossible to place in a mainstream journal of opinion. It was not until March 2004 that one could read in a US daily the news that the aid freeze might have contributed to the overthrow of the penniless Haitian government. In its one and only investigative piece about the three-year-long aid embargo, the *Boston Globe* finally stumbled upon the facts:

> WASHINGTON—For three years, the US government, the European Union, and international banks have blocked $500 million in aid to Haiti's government, ravaging the economy of a nation already twice as poor as any in the Western Hemisphere.
>
> The cutoff, intended to pressure the government to adopt political reforms, left Haiti struggling to meet even basic needs and weakened the authority of President Jean-Bertrand Aristide, who went into exile one week ago. Today, Haiti's government, which serves 8 million people, has an annual budget of about $300 million—less than that of Cambridge, [Massachusetts] a city of just over 100,000. And as Haitians attempt to form a new government, many say its success will largely depend on how much and how soon aid will flow to the country... Many of Aristide's supporters, in Haiti and abroad, angrily con-

tend that the international community, particularly the United States, abandoned the fledgling democracy when it needed aid the most. Many believe that Aristide himself was the target of the de facto economic sanctions, just as Haiti was beginning to put its finances back in order.

The Aristide Question

The view that the United States and France undermined Aristide is not a fringe opinion. Nobel Laureate and former president of Costa Rica Oscar Arias wrote in the *Washington Post* that, "in the case of Haiti, not only was the struggling democracy cut off from outside aid but an armed insurrection of former military and death-squad leaders was in the end endorsed by the US and French governments." The Caribbean nations grouped under CARICOM and the African Union have called for a formal investigation of Aristide's removal, and Gayle Smith, an Africa specialist on the National Security Council staff under President Bill Clinton, observed that "most people around the world believe that Aristide's departure was at best facilitated; at worst, coerced by the US and France."

Why such animus towards Haiti's leader from American and French officialdom? Answering this question helps reframe the one that is always asked by the press. Journalists never ask, for example, how much 150 million gold francs are worth today or what their loss might have meant for a struggling tropical economy. They ask, rather, "Is Aristide a good guy or a bad guy?" Certainly, Aristide is the sort of person who would and did say, "France extorted this money from Haiti by force and you should give it back to us so that we can build primary schools, primary health care, water systems, and roads." Aristide is also the sort of person who will do the math on the French debt, adding in interest and adjusting for inflation. He came up with a startling figure: France owes Haiti US$21,685,135,571.48 and counting, at five percent annual interest.

This figure was scoffed at by some French, the whole affair seen as some sort of comical farce mounted by their disgruntled former subjects; others in France, it's increasingly clear, were insulted or angered when the point was pressed in diplomatic and legal circles.

Aristide pressed the point. The figure of $21 billion was repeated again and again. The number 21 appeared all over the place in Haiti, along with the word "restitution." On January 1, 2004, during Haiti's bicentennial celebrations, Aristide announced he would replace a 21-gun salute with a litany of 21 points about what had been achieved in spite of the embargo and what would be done when restitution was made. The crowd went wild. The US and French press by and large dismissed his comments as silly, even though lawyers saw the case as not without legal merit.

It's hard to have even a brief conversation about Haiti without Aristide's personality coming up. What's more, it's usually easy to tell within minutes how one's interlocutor feels about him. Haiti is almost always referred to as polarized, but this is not true in every sense. Most Haitians have a lot in common: poverty, disease, mistrust of the great powers. Haiti's elections and polls, even recent ones, show that the poor majority still support Aristide. What's polarized are the middle classes and the traditional political elites—which together seem to constitute what human rights groups and political analysts term "civil society," a grouping that for some ineffable reason does not include the poor majority. Equally polarized are people like me: non-Haitians who concern themselves with that country's affairs for a whole host of reasons. Among those who can read and write, among the chattering classes, there is no more divisive figure than Aristide.

Given all the coups and assassination attempts and spectacular crimes mentioned above—given all the complexity—what is the standard storyline in the mainstream press? That Aristide had the chance to be "Haiti's Mandela," but instead "cruelly disappointed" his supporters who then defected in droves. Nothing could be further from the truth, as even a superficial review of the facts will show. First, Haiti is not South Africa. There can be no lofty figure who survives terrible mistreatment in order to lead his nation into the sunlit uplands of democracy because in order to preside over such transitions, or even to survive them, leaders have to be able to deliver on campaign promises. Haiti's legendary poverty makes this impossible without repatriated resources or access to credits and assistance. Aristide knew this, hence his attempts to free up development assistance for health, roads, water, and primary education. When outside assistance was blocked by Washington and Aristide's first strategy failed, the restitution of the French debt was moved to the fore.

This broader background helps explain why the two superpowers in the Caribbean region—the United States and France—are united on Haiti, if not on Iraq.

None of this is new, as even a cursory review of the past decade or so shows. On the eve of his 1990 election, under the banner headline "Front-Running Priest a Shock to Haiti," we read in the *New York Times* that "the former Salesian priest, long known for his strident brand of liberation theology, has sent profound shock waves through many of the sectors of this society that have traditionally made or broken presidents since Haiti's independence in 1804. From the business community, the army, and the Catholic and Protestant churches to Voodoo priests and rural landowners, sentiment is strongly, if not uniformly, set against him." In other words, everyone was always against Aristide—except the poor majority.

Between the coup that followed Aristide's inauguration and his return to Haiti, the coverage and debates were the same. Our nation's "paper of record" is especially revealing. On September 22, 1994, the *New York Times* ran a front-page piece about Aristide entitled "The Mouse That Roared." From it, we get a keen sense of Aristide as irritant: "The Clinton crowd has had to work hard to justify him to lawmakers who were unnerved by the October 1993 closed-door CIA briefing to Congress, in which the intelligence agency offered information—later proven false—that Father Aristide had received psychiatric treatment at a Montreal hospital in 1980. Senator Jesse Helms, Republican of North Carolina, left the briefing and branded him a 'psychopath'—a slur it has been hard for Father Aristide to get over."

It would be convenient for the traditional elite and other allies and overseas funders if Aristide, who has indeed been forced to preside over unimaginable penury, were to be abandoned by his own people. But what of suppressed Gallup polls, conducted with the hope of showing that Aristide is no longer popular? In fact, these 2002 polls indicate that Aristide is far and away Haiti's most popular and trusted politician. What is to be done about the Haitian voters who, to the horror of their elites and to the Republican right, keep voting for Aristide?

In truth, the protégés of Senator Jesse Helms have had more say in Aristide's fate than have the Haitian electorate. Aristide claims he had no idea where he was being taken on the night of February 28, 2004 until minutes before landing at, he was told, "a French military base." He found himself in the Central African Republic, a place he'd never visited before. Although US officials stated initially that he had been "taken to the country of his choice," Aristide's version of events surely seems more plausible. The Central African Republic is a country in not much more than name. About the size of Texas and with a population of only three million, it is subject to French military and economic interests. It is also, in spite of natural resources (diamonds, gold, oil, timber, and uranium) that any Haitian might envy, one of the world's poorest countries and highly unstable. A March 2003 BBC story reported that the capital, Bangui, was the world's most dangerous city. The United States has issued a travel advisory banning its citizens from traveling to the Central African Republic; our embassy there was closed two years ago. The Central African Republic "government" seized power in a military coup a little over a year ago.

When the poorly-briefed Aristide walked off the plane and across the tarmac, he found a single journalist waiting. What did he have to say after a 20-hour flight during which he did not know where he was bound? First, he thanked the Africans for their hospitality, and then he said only the following: "I declare in overthrowing me they have uprooted the trunk of the tree of peace, but it will grow back because the roots are Louverturian."

It's no surprise that Aristide would echo Toussaint Louverture, who is one of his heroes. In one of the few measured and informed pieces written about the current Haitian crisis, Madison Smartt Bell, writing in *Harper's Magazine*, linked the past to the present, as Haitians readily do:

> Toussaint did not live to see the result of his struggle: the emergence of Haiti as an independent black state, founded by slaves who had broken their own chains and driven off their masters. After his deportation to France, the torch he'd carried was passed to Jean-Jacques Dessalines, a man of more ferocious spirit, whose watchword was Koupe tet, boule kay— "Cut off heads and burn down houses." Papa Doc Duvalier had systematically associated himself and his regime with the spirit of Dessalines, as he deployed Dessalinien tactics on his own people: ruthless application of overwhelming force. Aristide seemed more attracted to the spirit of Toussaint, who had a real distaste for useless bloodshed, political and diplomatic skills to match or surpass his remarkable military talent, a delicately evolved sense of Haiti's relationship with the surrounding colonial powers, a devout Catholicism able to coexist with the Vodou [sic] he also practiced, and a social vision, based on harmonious cooperation among the races, a good two hundred years ahead of his time.

Bell observes that, in the end, "Toussaint was undone by foreign powers, and Aristide also had suffered plenty of vexation from outside interference." Since Bell's essay was published, Aristide is, like Toussaint, in something of a French prison.

The Who's Who

Who are the other players in these high-stakes games, games in which history weighs so heavily? For many years it's been the same cast of characters on both sides of the sea. Starting with the US dramatis personae helps to make things clearer on the Haitian side. The current Bush administration has put in charge of Latin American diplomacy two men who have been at it for a long time; their views are well-documented. As the "Special Presidential Envoy to the Western Hemisphere," Otto Reich is the United States' top diplomat in the region even though he has never survived a House or Senate hearing; he was appointed by Bush during a Congressional recess. In the 1990s, Reich was a lobbyist for industry (among his current deals: selling Lockheed-Martin fighter planes to Chile), but prior to that he had a long record of government service. In a recent *New Yorker* profile of Reich, William Finnegan gives us more background on his curriculum vitae:

> Reich first went to work for the Reagan Administration at the Agency for International Development, in 1981. As the civil war in Nicaragua heated up, he moved to the State Department, where, from 1983 to 1986, he headed a Contra-support program that operated out of an outfit called the Office of Public Diplomacy. The office arranged speeches and recommended books to public libraries, but it also leaked false stories to the press—that, for instance, the Sandinista government was receiving Soviet MiG fighters, or was involved in drug trafficking. A declassified memo from one of Reich's aides to Patrick Buchanan, the White House com-

munications director, boasted about the office's "White Propaganda" operations, including op-ed pieces prepared by its staff, signed by Contra leaders or academics, and placed in major newspapers. (Reich's spokesman denied this.) The office employed Army psychological-warfare specialists, and worked closely with Lieutenant Colonel Oliver North, at the National Security Council.

During the course of the Iran-Contra investigation, the US Comptroller General concluded that Reich's office had "engaged in prohibited, covert propaganda activities." But by then Otto Reich had been named US Ambassador to Venezuela, where he laid the groundwork for future efforts to destabilize President Hugo Chavez. Mind you, these are not all covert efforts: less than a year ago, Reich was on record hailing a coup against the left-leaning Chavez, urging the State department and opinion-makers—including the *New York Times*—to support "the new government." The *Times* complied. There was only one problem with this plan: the Venezuelan majority failed to fall into step. There was not adequate public support, in Venezuela or elsewhere in Latin America, for the coup, and so Chavez remained in his seat. Following Aristide's ouster, Chavez has promised that, should the US government try anything similar in Venezuela again, they will meet with two responses: an interruption in Venezuelan oil and another "hundred years' war" from all Latin Americans who respect self-determination and sovereignty.

When the Bush administration sent a certain Roger Noriega as its envoy to "work out" the Haitian crisis in February 2004, not everyone knew who he was, for Noriega's career has flourished in the back of Senate committees. For the better part of a decade, Noriega worked for Jesse Helms and his allies. Although it is no secret that Noriega has had Aristide in his sights for years, none of this history made it into the mainstream media until recently. Then things became clearer. On CNN on March 1, after Aristide's departure from Haiti, Congresswoman

Maxine Waters "accused Undersecretary of State for Latin America Roger Noriega—whom she called 'a Haiti hater'—of being behind the troubles there." The CNN report continued: "Noriega was a senior aide to former Senator Jesse Helms, who as chairman of the Senate Foreign Affairs Committee was a backer of longtime dictator Jean-Claude Duvalier and an opponent of Aristide."

When I share these biographical details and the names of other people who are driving these policies—I refer to Otto Reich, Jesse Helms, Jeane Kirkpatrick, Elliot Abrams, John Poindexter, Bush *père* and *fils*— and then mention Iran-Contra, Honduras, Venezuela, the Declaration of Quebec City, liberation theology, and the International Republican Institute, the Haiti story starts to hang together. Haiti policy is determined by a small number of people who were prominent in either Reagan's or George H.W. Bush's cabinets. Most are back in government today after an eight-year vacation in conservative think tanks, lobbying firms, and the like. Elliot Abrams, convicted of felony during the Iran-Contra hearings, serves on the National Security Council; Reagan's national-security advisor John Poindexter is now heading the Pentagon's counterterrorism office; John Negroponte, former Ambassador to Honduras, is now Ambassador to the United Nations. Jeane Kirkpatrick is on the board of the International Republican Institute, a prime source of funds for the political opposition to Aristide and, credible sources suggest, for the demobilized army personnel who provided the muscle for the Haitian opposition in early 2004. The far right of the US Republican party has been the key determinant of Haiti policy.

What about US Secretary of State Colin Powell? The Washington-based Council on Hemispheric Affairs, writing of events in Haiti, offers the following summary: "Powell's vision for Latin America is now indistinguishable from that of his junior hemispheric policymaking ideologues, Noriega and Reich. The battle for the Secretary of State's soul has ended in a rout for those who had highly regarded the man they thought he was, in contrast to the man he turned out to be."

On the Haitian side, naming the players is again a relatively easy exercise because they fall into a small set of categories. To sum up the opposition, you have Haiti's business elite, including those who own the Haitian media, and the former military and paramilitary— the very persons who were involved in the 1991-94 coup. Many were in jail for murder, drug trafficking, and crimes against humanity, and now every single one of them is free.

Among those released by the rebels is former General Prosper Avril, a leader of the notorious Presidential Guard under both François and Jean-Claude Duvalier. Avril seized power by a coup d'état in September 1988; he was deposed by another coup in March 1990. A US District Court found that Avril's regime had engaged in "a systematic pattern of egregious human rights abuses." It found him personally responsible for enough "torture and cruel, inhuman, or degrading treatment" to award six of his victims US$41 million in compensation. His victims included opposition politicians, union leaders, scholars, and even a doctor trying to practice community rural medicine. Avril's repression was not subtle: three torture victims were paraded on national television with faces grotesquely swollen, limbs bruised, and clothing covered with blood. He also suspended thirty-seven articles of the Constitution and declared a state of siege.

The US started protecting Avril shortly after the 1994 restitution of Haiti's elected leaders. In November, Secretary of State Warren Christopher relayed to the US Ambassador intelligence reports that the "Red Star Organization," under Mr. Avril's leadership, was "planning [a] harassment and assassination campaign directed at the Lavalas Party and Aristide supporters. The campaign is scheduled to commence in early December 1995"—right before the election that would allow Aristide to become the first president in Haitian history to peacefully hand over power to another elected civilian. This information was not passed on to the Haitian authorities, and that same month an assassination attempt was made against prominent Lavalas legislators. In December the Haitian police team investigating the case sought to arrest Mr. Avril at his home. A US Embassy official admitted that he had visited Avril the day before the arrest; immediately after the Haitian police arrived at Avril's house, US soldiers arrived. They tried to dissuade the Haitian police from making the arrest, and it was only after Haiti's president intervened personally on the police radio that the police were able to enter Avril's house. By the time they entered the premises he had fled to the neighboring residence of the Colombian ambassador. Police searching Avril's house found military uniforms, illegal police radios, and a cache of weapons.

Avril escaped to Israel but later returned to Haiti, where his international support and feared military capacity deterred further arrest attempts. He founded a political party, which has never fielded candidates for elections but was nevertheless invited by the International Republican Institute to participate in developing an opposition to Aristide. In May 2001, after US troops had withdrawn from Haiti and while Avril was at a book signing away from his home and his guns, the Haitian police finally seized the opportunity to execute Avril's arrest warrant. The successful arrest was greeted with applause by the vast majority of Haitians and by human rights and justice groups in Haiti, the United States, and Europe. Amnesty International asserted that the arrest "could mark a step forward by the Haitian justice system in its struggle against impunity," and that "the gravity of the human rights violations committed during General Avril's period in power, from his 1988 coup d'état to his departure in March 1990, cannot be ignored." France's Committee to Prosecute Duvalier concluded that "the General must be tried."

On December 9, 2003, the investigating magistrate in the

case of the Piatre Massacre, a March 1990 attack in which several peasants lost their lives, formally charged Avril in the case. He was in prison awaiting the termination of pre-trial proceedings when freed on March 2, 2004—the day after Aristide was deposed.

The list goes on. Rebel leader Guy Philippe is also a former soldier who received, during the last coup, training at a US military facility in Ecuador. When the army was demobilized, Philippe was incorporated into the new police force, serving as police chief in the Port-au-Prince suburb of Delmas and in the second-largest city, Cap-Haïtien. During his tenure, the United Nations International Civilian Mission learned that dozens of suspected gang members were summarily executed, mainly by police under the command of Philippe's deputy. The US Embassy has implicated Philippe in drug smuggling during his police career. These crimes, committed in large part by former military incorporated into the police force, are often pinned on Aristide even though he sought to prevent coup-happy human rights abusers from ending up in these posts in the first place.

Philippe fled Haiti in October 2000 when Haitian authorities discovered him plotting a coup, together with a clique of fellow police chiefs. Since that time, the Haitian government has accused Philippe of masterminding terrorist attacks on the Haitian Police Academy and the National Palace in July and December 2001, as well as lethal hit-and-run raids against police stations in Haiti's Central Plateau over the past two years.

In February 2004, Philippe's men bragged to the US press that they had executed Aristide supporters in Cap-Haïtien and Port-au-Prince, and many have indeed been reported missing. Philippe's declaration—"I am the chief, the military chief. The country is in my hands"—triggered the following response from Oscar Arias: "Nothing could more clearly prove why Haiti does not need an army than the boasting of rebel leader Guy Philippe last week in Port-au-Prince. The Haitian army was abolished nine years ago during a period of democratic transition, precisely to prevent the country from falling back into the hands of military men." On March 2, 2004, Philippe told the Associated Press that he would use his new powers to arrest constitutional Haiti's prime minister, Yvon Neptune, and he proceeded to lead a mob in an attack on Neptune's residence. Philippe has been quoted as saying that the man he most admires is Augusto Pinochet.

Louis-Jodel Chamblain was a sergeant in the Haitian army until 1989 or 1990. He reappeared on the scene in 1993 as one of the founders of the paramilitary group FRAPH. Formed during the 1991-94 military regime, FRAPH was responsible for numerous human rights violations before the 1994 restoration of democratic governance. Chamblain organized attacks against democracy supporters, issued FRAPH identity cards, and obtained official recognition for FRAPH from the dictatorship. Among the victims of FRAPH under Chamblain's leadership was Haitian Minister of Justice Guy Malary, ambushed and machine-gunned to death with his bodyguard and a driver on October 14, 1993. According to an October 28, 1993 CIA intelligence memorandum, "FRAPH members Jodel Chamblain, Emmanuel Constant, and Gabriel Douzable met with an unidentified military officer on the morning of 14 October to discuss plans to kill Malary." (Emmanuel "Toto" Constant, the leader of FRAPH, is now living as a free man in Queens, New York.)

In September 1995, Chamblain was among seven senior military and FRAPH leaders convicted in absentia and sentenced to forced labor for life for their involvement in the September 1993 extrajudicial execution of Antoine Izméry, a well-known pro-democracy activist. In November 2000, Chamblain was convicted in absentia in the Raboteau massacre trial. In late 1994 or early 1995, Chamblain went into exile to the Dominican Republic in order to avoid prosecution. He was regularly spotted in public by Haitian expatriates and international journalists.

All of these biographies have been a matter of public record for years, but one could mark the day—I marked it as

February 28, as the coup was unfolding—that the *New York Times* and other newspapers began offering a bit more background on the men who now control Latin America's oldest and most volatile nation. These sketches give an idea, too, of why the Haitian people were enthusiastic about demobilizing the army. Writing in the *Washington Post*, Oscar Arias underlined the degree of popular support for demilitarization: "Since Aristide said that he could not abolish the army without the support of the Haitian people, the Arias Foundation for Peace and Human Progress commissioned an independent polling firm to gauge popular support for the idea. The results were stunning: 62 percent of Haitians were strongly in favor of abolition and only 12 percent were against."

As for the traditional political elite, surely they're a mixed bag? Some have wanted to live in the National Palace, Haiti's executive mansion, since the time it was occupied by Papa Doc. Some are more marginal but just as destructive. When recently you saw one man destroying artwork on display in Port-au-Prince, you could read that he was a "pastor from the Party of God." In fact this man, a perennial presidential candidate, is delighted to burn, in full view of international cameras, precious objects linked with voodoo and other aspects of Haitian culture.

Who are these people? What unites them beyond their hatred of Aristide? They've all been around a long time but were not permitted to speak out or form political parties during the Duvalier or military dictatorships. One penetrating analysis, by an academic named Robert Maguire, noted that "we should remember that from the first day of Aristide's term, the opposition set up a provisional government. My own observation then was that things in Haiti had changed. This never would have been permitted before. It was a sign that Haiti seemed to be becoming a more tolerant place." Again, this is another social fact missed by the mainstream human rights groups.

The leaders of the Haitian "civil society" groups include U.S.-born André Apaid, the founder of a television station and owner of Alpha Corp., a garment manufacturer that was prominently featured in news reports about Disney's sweatshop suppliers. Aristide's relentless push to raise the minimum wage above 72 gourdes a day—about $1.60—cut into the massive profits of the offshore assembly industry, since its principal resource is the desperate joblessness of the Haitian population. The US Congress has passed a measure to build new garment factories in Haiti and encourage American companies to contract out more sweatshop labor—an answered prayer for Apaid.

As for the owners of the media in Haiti, they behave as owners often do when surrounded by the poor, the famished, and by *chimères*, described in the foreign press as armed thugs working for the Aristide government. But who are the *chimères*? Again, Madison Smartt Bell provides a better answer to this question than what we read in journalistic accounts or human rights reports:

> Before that term was coined, Haitian delinquent youths were called maleleve ("ill brought up") or, still more tellingly, sansmaman ("the motherless ones"). They were people who'd somehow reached adulthood without the nurture of the traditional lakou—communities that the combined forces of poverty and globalization had been shattering here for the last few decades. That was what made them so dangerous. The Chime were indeed chimeras; ill fortune left them as unrealized shadows. With better luck they might have been human beings, but they weren't. These were the people Aristide had originally been out to salvage; "Tout moun se moun" was his earliest motto ("Every man is a man").

Coup d'Etat as a Source of Amusement

This human salvage operation exploded in February 2004 as "rebels" continued to "take cities." I work in these towns and know the rebels' modus operandi. They came in, shot the police—who usually numbered no more than two or three—and left. Only a similarly equipped counterforce could have stopped them, and there you have it: Haiti has no army. But Haiti is no more Costa Rica, "the Switzerland of Central America," than it is South Africa. Haiti has so few friends. The beleaguered government appealed for help in the UN Security Council, but this was delayed by the Bush administration—delayed long enough for the government to fall or be pushed out.

Whatever we do learn about the events of February 2004, we know that the coup makes bemused commentary. The idea of the Central African Republic as Aristide's "country of choice" triggered good copy, certainly. One "news analysis" of these events in the *New York Times*, with a South African byline, reads as follows:

> Jean-Bertrand Aristide, Haiti's latest strongman-in-exile, wants to lick his wounds in South Africa, a land of world-beating beauty, Mediterranean weather, American-quality freeways and Paris-luxe shops fit for any deep-pocketed ex-ruler of an impoverished land. Instead, he whiles his days away in the Central African Republic, a Texas-size nation of flat plains, Amazonian humidity, just 400 miles of Afghan-quality paved roads and cheap butterfly-wing art at the capital's K-Cinq market. Contrast him with his most illustrious predecessor, Jean-Claude Duvalier, known as Baby Doc. Forced out of power in 1986 after 29 years, he now lives on the Côte d'Azur. If there is an art to landing a cushy post-dictatorial sinecure, Mr. Aristide seems to have mastered only part of it in his dozen years as Haiti's president—which began with his election but ended with his using increasingly forceful methods of rule. Perhaps he simply lacked the right stuff.

Some of the journalists writing about Haiti seem to lack the right stuff. Aristide has never been able to serve out as much as half of his elected term before being overthrown by military figures with close ties to the United States, notwithstanding the "dozen years as Haiti's president" cited by this reporter. And the attempt to line up Aristide with "deep-pocketed ex-rulers" relies on malicious inference belied by the facts.

Did the US and France have a hand in Aristide's forced removal? Were President and Mrs. Aristide being held in the Central African Republic against their will? How could they answer one way or another, being the guests of a government that threatened them after they criticized the United States and France in statements to friends and to the press? As the American lawyer for the government of Haiti put it, "Who can or will corroborate their story? The gardener? The janitor?" It is not that eyewitnesses are unavailable, but rather that few among them are willing to go on record against the US and France, and that when they do, their words are dismissed. One eyewitness report, from a "concierge" at the Aristide's home, was buried in *Libération*, a French daily: "In Creole, he tells a story that contradicts the official version, which says that the head of state freely accepted his departure. In a voice still haunted by fear, Joseph Pierre insists that the ex-president was kidnapped in the night between [Saturday and Sunday] by the American army: 'American white men came to get him in a helicopter. They took away his security guards too. It was around 2 in the morning. He didn't want to go. The American soldiers forced him to. Because they had their guns trained on him, he had to follow them. Only God is stronger than the Americans.'"

Perhaps. But most of Aristide's claims, initially disputed by US officials from Assistant Secretary of State Noriega to Donald Rumsfeld, are now acknowledged to be true. US claims that Aristide met with officials in Antigua—Aristide denied this—were undermined by reports from Antigua. After having claimed that the Aristides were taken to the "country of their choice," Noriega acknowledged during a House hearing that Aristide did not know of his destination until less than an hour before landing in the Central African Republic. Even officials there acknowledge that no Haitian authorities were involved in the choice of Aristide's destination.

Many more questions remain unanswered. We know that US funds overtly financed the opposition. But did they also fund, even indirectly, the rebellion that so prominently featured high-powered US weapons only a year after 20,000 such weapons were promised to the Dominican Republic army? Senator Christopher Dodd is urging an investigation of US training sessions of 600 "rebels" in the Dominican Republic and also wants to investigate "how the International Republican Institute spent $1.2 million of tax payer money" in Haiti. Answering these and related questions will require an intrepid investigative reporter willing to take on hard questions about US policies in Latin America.

Oscar Arias concludes that, "were the international community now to stand by as the rebels reinstated the army, it would surely destroy the seeds of peace and self-rule that have been planted with great sacrifice by the Haitian people." But about the return of the military, there can be little doubt. The man sworn as Haiti's new prime minister announced in his first public statement that Aristide's order to replace the military with a civilian police force violated Haiti's constitution; he promised to name a commission to examine the issues surrounding its restoration. The de facto prime minister also named a former general to his new government.

More guns and more military may well be the time-honored prescription for policing poverty, but violence and chaos will not go away if the Haitian people's hunger, illness, poverty, and disenfranchisement are not addressed.

CHAPTER THREE

Rep. Maxine Waters Charges US Is Encouraging A Coup*

Monday, February 16th, 2004

Several thousand demonstrators clashed with supporters of Haitian President Jean-Bertrand Aristide this weekend as they marched through the streets of the capital Port-au-Prince. We speak with Rep. Maxine Waters (D-CA) about what role the US is playing in the current events in the country.

In Haiti, anti-government gangs and militias are working with opposition groups and former army officers in an effort to overthrow the government of Jean Bertrand Aristide. There is concern that Washington is once again working behind the scenes to foment a coup.

For weeks, Haiti has seen armed gangs attacking government forces and supporters in various towns and cities across the country. Pro-government supporters have been defending Aristide. There have been a series of armed battles that have resulted in at least 40 deaths. Haiti has no army and has a dwindling police force numbering only a few thousand.

On Sunday, several thousand demonstrators clashed with Aristide supporters as they marched through the streets of the capital, Port-au-Prince. Police used tear gas to keep the two sides apart.

Meanwhile, Prime Minister Yvon Neptune told the BBC

---

*In the following chapters, the reports and transcrpts from Democracy Now! provide an on-the-ground assessment as events unfolded.

that the government planned to launch an attack to regain control of Gonaives, the fourth-largest city in Haiti. Anti-government gangs are thought to control about 11 towns and cities across the country.

• Rep. Maxine Waters, Democratic Congresswoman from California serving in her seventh term. She is the Chief Deputy Whip of the Democratic Party and serves as Co-Chair of the House Democratic Steering Committee. She is the former chair of the Congressional Black Caucus. She recently returned from Haiti.

AMY GOODMAN: We are joined on the telephone right now by congress member Maxine Waters who is from Los Angeles serving in her seventh term. She is Chief Deputy Whip of the Democratic Party. co-chair of the House Democratic Steering Committee and former chair of the Congressional Black Caucus. She has just returned from Haiti. Welcome to Democracy Now!

MAXINE WATERS: Thank you very much.

AMY GOODMAN: It's good to have you with us. What is your assessment of what's happening?

MAXINE WATERS: Well, I think the introduction that you just made is basically correct. We have somewhat of a crisis there, where you have this opposition that is supported, I believe, by Mr. Noriega in the State Department, and others who have always had their hands in the politics of Haiti. Who are trying to oust the president. And these so-called peaceful marches are not peaceful. They are creating the violence, and Aristide is being blamed for the violence that's being created by—by Andy Apaid and the so-called committee group of 184. Gonaives is an important place in Haiti and it has been under the control of these thugs that have been supported by FRAPH. And also some of the opposition that claims not to be violent. And the president is going to have to do something about it. He cannot just allow these thugs and the opposition to take over

these cities and towns. He has been very patient. He has asked
them to put down their guns. He has asked the opposition to
come to the table. They have refused, despite the fact that
everybody has gotten behind the CARICOM Proposal as a way
to bring people to the table, but Andy Apaid and the group of
184 refuse to negotiate. So, the president has no choice but to
try and stabilize Gonaives and some of these areas, and to get
the thugs out, and to try to get the United States to stop this
backing of these thugs and this opposition. He needs some help.
The police department force is down to about 3,000 or more,
and that's a country of over 8 million, about 8 million people.
So, the United States, the World Bank, the International
Monetary Fund, O.A.S., people should sit down and honestly
try and be of assistance to Haiti. It's a very unfortunate situation.

AMY GOODMAN: What evidence do you have that the
US government is supporting the anti-Aristide forces?

MAXINE WATERS: Well, I guess a few days ago there
was an article that appeared in the *New York Times* with a so-
called anonymous—someone in the State Department having,
you know, sent a trial balloon up saying that something was
going to have to be done in Haiti, and it was possible that the
State Department could support the ouster. Well, not only did
you see that kind of a statement coming out of the State
Department, I noticed that each of the releases that they had
done over the past several weeks kept suggesting that everything that was going on, all of the problems were the fault of the
president, and they were literally giving out misinformation.
Well, Mr. Noriega, of course, was the chief of staff to Senator
Jesse Helms, who was basically a Haiti—well, hated Haiti, and
they have always worked against Haiti, and Mr. Noriega, is now
in charge of that policy. And I think it's because of him—I really believe it's because of him that these statements keep coming
out of the State Department, and I think that Colin Powell was
focused on Afghanistan and Iraq, and I have been communi-

cating with him recently, and I have asked him to pay more attention. I have talked to him about Andy Apaid, who is leading the group of 184. And the latest statement from him that came out of the State Department was much more balanced. I am hopeful that he will move Noriega out of the way so that we can get behind the CARICOM proposal and try to make sense out of it and give help. It appears that that's the direction that Colin Powell is moving in.

AMY GOODMAN: We know the history of the United States in the previous coup in Haiti. Aristide forced out for three years, 1991 to 1994. It turned out that the leader of the paramilitary death squad, the FRAPH, Emmanuel Constance was on the payroll of the Defense Intelligence Agency, and as President Clinton was saying we have to go off the murderers and the rapists and thugs in Haiti, justifying why the US was moving in. It turned out on his own government's payroll was the leader that he was talking about. And now he walks free in the United States, most likely here in New York in Queens.

MAXINE WATERS: Yes, that is true. He is on the streets of New York. And that sad history is a history that we in America are ashamed of. Not only have we supported dictators in Haiti, Papa Doc and Baby Doc Duvalier. The CIA has always had a hand. And we've had people like Constance on the payroll. I really believe that despite the fact that we worked very, very hard to get President Clinton involved in Haiti, and supporting the return of President Aristide to Haiti, as someone said yesterday, the job was not finished. What we did was simply put him back there, but we have allowed the embargo against Haiti to literally choke that country, not only has he not gotten the support from the State Department, the World Bank removed itself, basically, from Haiti. It took us years to get the IDB to pay attention, and to appropriate the dollars [that had supported for Haiti,] and still that money has not gotten to the government. They're still waiting on certain conditions to be met. So, president Clinton, even though he certainly did do the right thing, we should have stayed longer. In support of Haiti. We should have given more support to the training, and development and expansion of the police force, and so, the job was just half done. They're at great risk now.

CHAPTER FOUR

Haitian Prime Minister:
"Coup d'Etat Machine in Motion"
Wednesday, February 18th, 2004

Haitian Prime Minister Yvon Neptune said international assistance was needed after nearly two weeks of violence in Haiti orchestrated by opponents of the government has left dozens of people dead. UN Secretary General Kofi Annan is considering taking some role in the country and France said it would consider sending peacekeepers.

Haitian Prime Minister Yvon Neptune said yesterday "We are witnessing the coup d'état machine in motion." Neptune said international assistance was needed after nearly two weeks of violence orchestrated by opponents of the government had left dozens of people dead.

Agence France Presse reports that United Nations Secretary General Kofi Annan is considering taking some role in the country and France said it would consider sending peacekeepers. Meanwhile the White House publicly urged President Aristide to take, "essential steps" to change how he governs the nation.

- Kim Ives, editor of the Haitian newspaper, *Haiti Progres*.

AMY GOODMAN: We are on the line with Kim Ives editor of *Haiti Progres*. What's happening in the country right now?

KIM IVES: Amy, it's looking like Congo, 1960. You know, it's a former colonial and slave-owning power fomenting a rebellion against President Aristide just as they did back then. And we see, in fact, wealthy businessmen leading the rebellion against the government much like the Congo. And we see

Aristide on the verge of requesting peacekeepers; again as Lamumba did, but we know in the case of the Congo, that UN Peacekeepers that came in disarmed Lamumba's troops helping the rebellion against them and in the end result there was a coup by Mobutu, which turned him over to his killers. We're hoping that scenario is not reproducing. We see France, Haiti's colonial master, saying it's ready to act to come in. Sending an intervention force. This is the same country that has been fomenting the rebellion over the past months. Its French diplomats who have been funding the principle opposition radio station in Haiti, who have been chaperoning and supporting the opposition leaders in trips around the country, and marches. Now they're claiming they're coming to help resolve the situation. It's a little unclear whether France is working independently or is a surrogate for the US We know that between these two powers, the Caribbean is seen as the U.S.'s backyard. This is something Washington has done often. It pushes Canada and France, the two other principle powers with influence in Haiti and economic interests to the fore, while they hang back. I don't think people should take the declarations of secretary of State Colin Powell, who says there's "no enthusiasm for an intervention." On the contrary, we feel that the US has had the heaviest hand in the affairs of Haiti. I have been trying to bring it precisely to this point where they can point to anarchy in the country and say, clearly, these are people who cannot govern themselves, and they need foreign intervention.

AMY GOODMAN: Kim, what about the former coup leaders, people like Earl Cedras, people like Emmanuel Constance, who was on the head of the US intelligence agency payroll, fomenting the coup from 1991 to 1994?

KIM IVES: Now, we see Toto Constance, who is presently, we believe, at least, enjoying a golden political asylum here in Queens, New York.

AMY GOODMAN: Is there any sign that any of them are returning to Haiti?

KIM IVES: Yes. Indeed. The number two of the FRAPH organization, Louis Jordel who showed up last week at the head of a column of all-terrain vehicles and guys dressed in camouflage gear with rifles. He led the assault on the town of Heche, where the police chief and his bodyguard were killed in the assaults. They emptied the prison. As they do in each case when they take a town. Often recruiting troops from the convicts. And then they burn down the police station. So, now Chambleir is in it. And if you want prove that terrorists are involved in the uprising, you have it right there.

AMY GOODMAN: I thank you for being with us. We will continue to follow the story in Haiti very closely. This is Democracy Now!

CHAPTER FIVE

Haiti's Lawyer: US Is Arming Anti-Aristide Paramilitaries

Amy Goodman and Jeremy Scahill
Wednesday, February 25th, 2004

As opponents of Haitian President Aristide reject a U.S.-brokered peace plan, we speak with Ira Kurzban who has served as General Counsel for the government of Haiti since 1991.

The US lawyer representing the government of Haiti charged today that the US government is directly involved in a military coup attempt against the country's democratically elected President, Jean-Bertrand Aristide. Ira Kurzban, the Miami-based attorney who has served as General Counsel to the Haitian government since 1991, said that the paramilitaries fighting to overthrow Aristide are being backed by Washington.

"I believe that this is a group that is armed by, trained by, and employed by the intelligence services of the United States," Kurzban told the national radio and TV program Democracy Now! "This is clearly a military operation, and it's a military coup."

"There's enough indications from our point of view, at least from my point of view, that the United States certainly knew what was coming about two weeks before this military operation started," Kurzban said. "The United States made contingency plans for Guantanamo."

If a direct US connection is proven, it will mark the second time in just over a decade that Washington has been involved in a coup in Haiti.

Several of the paramilitary leaders now rampaging Haiti are men who were at the forefront of the US-backed campaign of terror during the 1991-94 coup against Aristide. Among the paramilitary figures now leading the current insurrection is Louis Jodel Chamblain, the former number two man in the FRAPH paramilitary death squad.

Chamblain was convicted and sentenced in absentia to hard-labor for life in trials for the April 23, 1994 massacre in the pro-democracy region of Raboteau and the September 11, 1993 assassination of democracy-activist Antoine Izméry. Chamblain recently arrived in Gonaives with about 25 other commandos based in the Dominican Republic, where Chamblain has been living since 1994. They were well equipped with rifles, camouflage uniforms, and all-terrain vehicles.

Among the victims of FRAPH under Chamblain's leadership was Haitian Justice Minister Guy Malary. He was ambushed and machine-gunned to death with his bodyguard and a driver on October 14, 1993. According to an October 28, 1993 CIA Intelligence Memorandum obtained by the Center for Constitutional Rights "FRAPH members Jodel Chamblain, Emmanuel Constant, and Gabriel Douzable met with an unidentified military officer on the morning of 14 October to discuss plans to kill Malary." Emmanuel "Toto" Constant, was the founder of FRAPH.

An October 1994 article by journalist Allan Nairn in *The Nation* magazine quoted Constant as saying that he was contacted by a US Military officer named Col. Patrick Collins, who served as defense attaché at the United States Embassy in Port-au-Prince. Constant says Collins pressed him to set up a group to "balance the Aristide movement" and do "intelligence" work against it. Constant admitted that, at the time, he was working with CIA operatives in Haiti. Constant is now residing freely in the US He is reportedly living in Queens, NY. At the time, James Woolsey was head of the CIA.

Another figure to recently reemerge is Guy Philippe, a former Haitian police chief who fled Haiti in October 2000 after authorities discovered him plotting a coup with a group of other police chiefs. All of the men were trained in Ecuador by US Special Forces during the 1991-1994 coup. Since that time, the Haitian government has accused Philippe of master-minding deadly attacks on the Police Academy and the National Palace in July and December 2001, as well as hit-and-run raids against police stations on Haiti's Central Plateau over the following two years.

Kurzban also points to the presence of another FRAPH veteran, Jean Tatoune. Along with Chamblain, Tatoune was convicted of gross violations of human rights and murder in the Raboteau massacre.

"These people came through the Dominican border after the United States had provided 20,000 M-16s to the Dominican army," says Kurzban. "I believe that the United States clearly knew about it before, and that given the fact of the history of these people, [Washington is] probably very, very deeply involved, and I think Congress needs to seriously look at what the involvement of the Defense Intelligence Agency and the Central Intelligence Agency has been in this operation. Because it is a military operation. It's not a rag-tag group of liberators, as has often been put in the press in the last week or two."

Kurzban says he has hired military analysts to review photos of the weapons being used by the paramilitary groups. He says that contrary to reports in the media that the armed groups are using weapons originally distributed by Aristide, the gangs are using highly sophisticated and powerful weapons; weapons that far out-gun Aristide's 3,000 member National Police force.

"I don't think that there's any question about the fact that the weapons that they have did not come from Haiti," says Kurzban. "They're organized as a military commando strike force that's going from city to city."

Kurzban says that among the weapons being used by the paramilitaries are: M-16s, M-60s, armor piercing weapons and rocket-propelled grenade launchers. "They have weapons to shoot down the one helicopter that the government has," he said. "They have acted as a pretty tight-knit commando unit."

Chamblain and other paramilitary leaders have said they will march on the capital, Port-au-Prince, within two weeks. The US has put forth a proposal, being referred to as a peace plan, that many viewed as favorable to Aristide's opponents. Aristide accepted the plan, but the opposition rejected it. Washington's point man on the crisis is Roger Noriega, Undersecretary of State for Western Hemispheric Affairs.

"I think Noriega has been an Aristide hater for over a decade," says Kurzban, adding that he believes Noriega allowed the opposition to delay their response to the plan to allow the paramilitaries to capture more territory. "My reaction was they're just giving them more time so they can take over more, that the military wing of the opposition can take over more ground in Haiti and create a fait accompli," Kurzban said. "Indeed, as soon as they said, 'we need an extra day,' I predicted, unfortunately, and correctly, that they would go into Cap Haitian (Haiti's second largest city) and indeed the next morning they did."

The leader of the "opposition" is an American citizen named Andy Apaid. He was born in New York. Haitian law does not allow dual-nationality and he has not renounced his US citizenship. In a recent statement, Congressmember Maxine Waters blasted Apaid and his opposition front, saying she believes "Apaid is attempting to instigate a bloodbath in Haiti and then blame the government for the resulting disaster in the belief that the United States will aid the so-called protestors against President Aristide and his government."

"We have the leader of the opposition, who Mr. Noriega is negotiating with, who Secretary Powell calls and who tells Secretary Powell, you know, 'we need a couple more days' and

Secretary Powell says 'that's fine,'" says Kurzban. "I mean, there's some kind of theater of the absurd going on with this opposition where it's led by an American citizen, where they're just clearly stalling for time until they can get more ground covered in Haiti through their military wing, and the United States and Noriega, with a wink and nod, is kind of letting them do that."

Kurzban says that because Aristide's opponents rejected Washington's plan, "the next step clearly is to send in some kind of UN peacekeeping force immediately."

"The question is," says Kurzban. "Will the international community stand by and allow a democracy in this hemisphere to be terminated by a brutal military coup of persons who have a very, very sordid history of gross violations of human rights?"

AMY GOODMAN: We're going to start with Ira Kurzban, a Miami-based lawyer. Since 1991, he served as General Counsel for the government of Haiti. Welcome to Democracy Now!.

IRA KURZBAN: Good morning.

AMY GOODMAN: It's good to have you with us. What is your assessment of what's happening in Haiti right now?

IRA KURZBAN: Well, I think this is clearly a military operation, and it's a military coup. We have analyzed the kinds of weapons that these people have brought from the Dominican Republic, who they are, how they're organized, and they're organized, really, as a military commando strike force that's going from city to city. They're very well organized, and they're armed to the teeth with the kinds of weapons, Amy, that really, no one has ever seen in Haiti, except when Haiti had an army. This notion that somehow, you know, this is kind of a rag-tag group of people who had arms that they got originally from Aristide, which is kind of what's playing in the press generally, is just totally untrue. When we have looked at the weapons that they have, they have M-16s, M-60s. They now have armor piercing weapons they have rocket propelled launchers. They have weapons to shoot down the one helicopter that the government has. They have acted as a pretty tight-knit commando unit, and they're led by, as I think you were pointing out in the introduction—they're led by people who were former associates of the Defense Intelligence Agency. Jodel Chamblin was the trigger man for FRAPH during the military coup, when FRAPH was a creation of the Defense Intelligence Agency of the United States. There's enough indications from our point of view, at least from my point of view, that the United States certainly knew what was coming about two weeks before this military operation started.

The US Ambassador in Port-au-Prince began the process of warning American citizens and asking them to register. This was a week before any of this, and two weeks before any of this happened. So, there was a clear feeling that something was going to happen, and what really happened is the combination of Jean Tatun who is a person that the press has rarely reported about in Gonaives, who was a former FRAPH person who we tried and convicted for gross violations of human rights and murder in Raboteau, and is behind what's going on in Gonaives. He had strong connections with Chamblain, the ex-head of FRAPH, and Guy Philippe, a former member of the Haitian armed forces who has attempted previous coups, not only against Aristide, but the Preval government. These people came through the Dominican border after the United States had provided 20,000 M-16s to the Dominican army. They came through the border, that is Philippe and Chamblain with a really small army of about 20 or 30 highly trained military people with these M-16s and M-60s and all of this other equipment that came through the Dominican border with—in several trucks with very, very heavy equipment.

And quite frankly, I believe that the United States clearly knew about it before, and that given the fact of the history of these people, we are probably very, very deeply involved, and I think Congress needs to seriously look at what the involvement of the Defense Intelligence Agency and the Central Intelligence Agency has been in this operation. Because it is a military operation. It's not a rag-tag group of liberators, as has often been put in the press in the last week or two.

The second part of it is that it's clear that as a result of a number of stories that have come out in the last two days that the so-called peaceful opposition has been working very, very closely with these people. Guy Philippe was quoted in the Associated Press yesterday saying with a big smile on his face that he has not been officially in contact with the opposition, but that he has received money and support from the Haitian business community. Well, the Haitian business community are the people who are behind what's called the group of 184. Those are the people who were so-called peaceful opposition. It's clear to us that their stalling tactics in the last week have been designed to develop a fait accompli on the ground. I think that's what we're seeing right now.

AMY GOODMAN: Ira Kurzban, you're saying that you believe that the US is arming the opposition and did it through sending weapons to Dominican Republic, which were then given over to the opposition and came across the border?

IRA KURZBAN: That's right. I don't think that there's any question about the fact that the weapons that they have did not come from Haiti. They clearly came over the Dominican border when Philippe and Chamblain entered Haiti about two weeks ago.

AMY GOODMAN: Hadn't Guy Philippe been arrested in the Dominican Republic at one time?

IRA KURZBAN: Yes. Guy Philippe was heavily involved in drug dealing in Cap-Haitien and was involved in a coup against Preval. And the reason I point that out is because a lot of the press reports are saying this is all about Aristide and so forth. It has nothing really to do with Aristide. This is a military operation designed to bring back the Haitian army. And I think that the US Defense Intelligence Agency has always wanted to push to have the army reconstituted. So Philippe was involved in a coup in the year 2000 against President Preval and the thrust of that then, just as the thrust of it now is, we want to bring back the Haitian Army. So under the cover of this is all about Aristide and how undemocratic he has been and so forth, it's really an operation to bring back the army. When he tried the coup in 2000 he was fired from the police and fled to the Dominican Republic and the Haitian government has made many efforts to extradite him and to put him on trial as a result of not only that effort but what happened on December 17 where one of his cohorts readily admitted that Philippe and his cohorts were involved in a coup to take the National Palace.

They have tried this two or three times in different ways. There was an effort in July of 2001 to capture the police stations in Haiti, and that was unsuccessful. There was another effort on December 17 to take the National Palace, and that was unsuccessful. And obviously, they have regrouped. They have obtained these kinds of very, very heavy weapons. And are coming across the border. Yes, to be perfectly clear, Amy, I believe that this is a group that is armed by, trained by, and employed by the intelligence services of the United States. I think that the Congress really needs to take a very careful look at this now.

AMY GOODMAN: Do you expect to see Port-au-Prince fall to the opposition forces, heavily armed in the next few days? Is Aristide expecting this? Is Aristide expecting to be forced out again?

IRA KURZBAN: The president went on national TV in Haiti and also spoke with the international community yesterday saying what's really going on about this military coup and asking for international assistance. I mean, the Haitians who are in Port-au-Prince and the police who have acted very, very valiantly against very difficult odds and the palace security are all prepared to fight, and I think they will fight. I don't think that you are going to see the situation that you have seen in some other places where they—this military operation has been able to roll into the cities because of their disproportionate fire power. And one thing I think that needs to be made clear, Amy, in this is when the press reports that these people easily went into the city because there's so much opposition to Aristide, I think it's really doing a disservice to the American public because what's happening is people are trying to fight back with machetes and rocks and bottles, and they're facing M-60s which are the weapon that Rambo had in the movie. I mean, these are huge, powerful weapons against people who are trying to stand up for democracy and of course, you know, they are—they have not been able to stop this well-armed and well-trained group of commandos.

And I think the situation, though, in Port-au-Prince is very different. There are many, many police now in Port-au-Prince. There are security forces in Port-au-Prince. I think they're prepared to fight. I think they will fight. I think the president, and really being a statesman, is trying to say to the world, we need to stop this. You know, this is the 21st century. Haiti should be moving forward. We should be moving forward toward peace. We should resolve this in a peaceful way. There's going to be a lot of bloodshed and with bloodshed, there's also going to be boat people who are going to be fleeing the country in the next six months or a year. If these guys do take over, they're bad actors. These are people who were killers and even as the Secretary of State acknowledged, thugs and criminals who have a very, very bad human rights history in Haiti.

AMY GOODMAN: Roger Noriega led the delegation to Haiti to broker the peace plan, the former aide to Jesse Helms. What do you think his role in this is, Ira Kurzban?

IRA KURZBAN: I think Noriega has been an Aristide hater for over a decade. I would like to think that he was really trying to broker a sincere agreement, but when I saw what happened, and I was there on Saturday before the President almost immediately agreed, after an hour or two discussion, to the peace plan where it would clearly result in his having to share power with people who have been his bitter enemies for a long time and then the opposition said we needed several more days, and you know, Noriega and the others were willing to give it to them, my reaction was they're just giving them more time so they can take over more, that the military wing of the opposition can take over more ground in Haiti and create a fait accompli and indeed, as soon as they said, we need an extra day, I predicted, unfortunately, and correctly, that they would go into Cap Haitian and indeed the next morning they did.

The thing that's peculiar and I don't think Americans understand this, the leader of the opposition, Andy Apaid, is an American citizen. He is not a Haitian citizen, because Haiti does not recognize dual nationality. One must choose either their Haitian citizenship or their US citizenship. He has never renounced his US citizenship. We have the leader of the opposition, who Mr. Noriega is negotiating with, who Secretary Powell calls and who tells Secretary Powell, "you know, we need a couple more days" and Secretary Powell says that's fine. I mean, there's some kind of theater of the absurd going on with this opposition where it's led by an American citizen, where they're just clearly stalling for time until they can get more ground covered in Haiti through their military wing, and the United States and Noriega with a wink and nod as kind of letting them do that. Now they have said no. Presumably if the US is serious, about what Secretary Powell said in preserving democracy and allowing President Aristide to fulfill his term, he agreed to the peace plan. They have not. The next step clearly is to send in some kind of UN peacekeeping force immediately.

AMY GOODMAN: It's interesting that you said that Secretary of State Colin Powell called them, what did you say, criminals and thugs.

IRA KURZBAN: Thugs.

AMY GOODMAN: Because when President Clinton announced that the US was going to be moving in, to challenge the coup of 1991-94, he talked about them as murderers and rapists and criminals. Meanwhile, Emmanuel Constant, the head of the FRAPH at the time was on the payroll of the Defense Intelligence Agency. This is when James Woolsey was the head of the CIA. On the one hand, you have the president attacking them and on the other hand, you have the people leading the coup on the US payroll.

IRA KURZBAN: I think that there is—as I said before, I believe that Congress should certainly look at, and investigate what the role of the Defense Intelligence Agency and the CIA is here. You know, I personally believe that they are involved, given the history, given the nature of the weapons that these people have, and given that their major demand is the return of the Haitian army, even more than anything—any other demand they have made in the last two weeks, and given these long-standing ties. So, yeah, it's true that the Secretary has said what he said, and we hope that he is sincere in saying that. And we hope that he is going to act on it now, and that the administration is going to act on it. The President of Haiti facing a military coup, has now said, we need international assistance. He said it to the world yesterday. And the question is, will the world act or will they allow a democracy to be destroyed. No one has ever contested that President Aristide's election was not a full, fair election and no one has ever said that Aristide would not have been elected in the year 2000 because of his overwhelming popularity. The question is will the international community stand by and allow a democracy in this hemisphere to be terminated by a brutal military coup of persons who have a very, very sordid history and gross violations of human rights.

AMY GOODMAN: Ira Kurzban, lawyer for the Haitian government.

CHAPTER SIX

Haiti: Different Coup, Same Paramilitary Leaders*

Thursday, February 26th, 2004

For a closer look at what is happening right now on the ground in Haiti, we look back at the involvement of the US in the 1991-1994 coup period with veteran investigative journalist Allan Nairn who broke a number of stories that proved the direct links between US intelligence agencies and Haitian paramilitary death squads in the early 1990s.

Many of the men leading the armed insurrection in Haiti right now are well known to veteran Haiti observers and, for that matter, the US intelligence agencies that worked closely with the paramilitary death squads which terrorized Haiti in the early 1990s. People like Louis Jodel Chamblain, the former number two man in FRAPH, Guy Philippe, a former police chief who was trained by US Special Forces in Ecuador and Jean Tatoune, another leader of FRAPH.

In an hour-long interview with the *Washington Post*, published today Guy Philippe vowed a bloody assault on Port-au-Prince "very soon" if Aristide refuses to leave office. Philippe and Chamblain told the paper that Aristide's departure and his replacement by an interim leader who would call new elections was the only possible peaceful solution to their three-week-old insurgency. Chamblain said "Aristide has two choices: prison or

---

*With Juan Gonzalez, co-host of Democracy Now!

execution by firing squad."

Preparations against a possible assault by the paramilitaries were evident in Port-au-Prince. Pro-Aristide militia groups stepped up their vigilance in the increasingly tense capital, setting up roadblocks and burning tires after dark at intersections throughout the city. Vehicles throughout the city are being stopped and searched.

Philippe said some of his forces are already in Port-au-Prince, some, he said, undercover in the National Palace. He predicted that they would use intelligence to identify and locate leaders of pro-Aristide groups, "neutralize them" and take the city in "one or two hours." He said his forces would kill Aristide if he resisted an attack, but that a trial would be preferable, either in Haiti or at an international court. Philippe said he would welcome an international peacekeeping force, provided Aristide was gone.

For a closer look at what is happening right now on the ground in Haiti, we are going to look back at the involvement of the US in the 1991-1994 coup period.

- Allan Nairn, a veteran investigative journalist, he was in Haiti during the 1991-94 coup and broke a number of stories that proved the direct links between US intelligence agencies and Haitian paramilitary death squads. Among the stories he broke was that the head of FRAPH, Emmanuel "Toto" Constant, was on the payroll of the Defense Intelligence Agency.

AMY GOODMAN: We're joined now by Allan Nairn, an investigative journalist and activist in Haiti during the 1991-94 coup period. He won the George Polk award for stories that proved the direct links between US intelligence agencies and Haitian paramilitary death squads. Among the stories he broke was that the man who launched FRAPH, Emmanuel "Toto" Constant, was on the payroll of the Defense Intelligence Agency. Allan Nairn, welcome to Democracy Now!. Let me start by asking, is it proper to say that Constant launched FRAPH, or did US intelligence agencies?

ALLAN NAIRN: Well, Constant did with the support of the DIA and also the CIA.

AMY GOODMAN: Can you talk about that period? Can you talk about the relationship when President Clinton went on the national airwaves and announced that the US military was going to move in, to go after the murderers, and the thugs, and the rapists, those who were doing this on the ground in Haiti. What was their relationship with the US government?

ALLAN NAIRN: Well, many of them were on the pay-roll of the US government. Historically, the US had backed oppressive forces in Haiti for centuries. France plundered the wealth of Haiti. After that, when there wasn't much left, even though there wasn't much left to plunder, the US backed a series of repressive regimes. Under the Duvaliers, through Israel, the US funded massive military and intelligence aid. And after Baby Doc Duvalier was brought down by a popular uprising, the US continued to back the paramilitary forces. Starting around 1989, the US Defense Intelligence Agency encouraged the for-mation of FRAPH, essentially a terrorist group. Colonel Patrick Collins, the defense attache began working with Constant. And Constant was later placed on the CIA payroll. He received cash payments from John Kambourian, the CIA Station Chief. Also one of the key leaders of the coup that ousted Aristide from his democratically elected presidency, the first time around, Michelle Francois, was also on the payroll according to a CIA— the CIA payroll according to a US State Department official I interviewed. So, many of the officials whom Clinton was claim-ing to be fighting, were actually his employees, and if at that time, Clinton had simply cut them off, completely ended their support, the Haitian public itself most likely could have brought down the coup regime without a US occupation.

The price of that US occupation was that before Aristide was brought back, he was essentially forced to agree to abandon the economic program of the popular movement, a program of redistributing wealth from the rich to the poor. Aristide was pressured by Clinton and his National Security Adviser, Anthony Lake, to sign on to a World Bank-IMF program, which in the words of one of the main authors of that program, would redistribute some wealth from the poor to the rich. Aristide agreed to that, in part because he saw that while he was in exile in the United States, his people were being killed on the ground by FRAPH and by the people of Francois and the coup regime. And when Aristide came back under those conditions, in a US helicopter, moving around surrounded by US Special Forces people, cut off, to a great extent, from the popular movement, it was really the beginning of the end of the popular movement in Haiti, and also, I think, the beginning of Aristide's own corruption, which helped lead to this current crisis.

JUAN GONZALEZ: Allan, you mentioned John Kambourian, the former CIA Station Chief, but I recall being back in the early 1990s in Haiti covering the events. I will never forget the day before the USS *Harlan County*, which President Clinton and the UN were sending in peacekeepers in the fall of 1993 and I happened to be with the Daily News reporter at a restaurant in Patienville with some of the top anti-Aristide elite there, including the number two person in the port, who assured me, and our reporter, and my photographer that the *Harlan County* was not going to land next day, that everything had been arranged. I told him, "What do you mean? President Clinton is sending them in." And as we were sitting there in the restaurant in walks John Kambourian and sits down at our table and begins to huddle with the number two man at the port and various other officials. The next morning, sure enough as the business people had predicted, the *Harlan County* was stopped and blocked at the gate by a FRAPH crew and there's John Kambourian, serenely watching the whole situation unfold. I bumped into him on a plane ride a few weeks later, and I said, "Weren't you worried about these FRAPH people?" And he said, "Oh, they don't mean any harm, they're harmless." So it was clear that he was well aware of everything that was going on with the attempt to push back the *Harlan County* that day.

ALLAN NAIRN: That seemed to have been the case of one hand not knowing what the other was doing. Here you had one US force being interfered with by the FRAPH people, who were being backed by another. But what the first Bush administration and then Clinton did in backing FRAPH was they backed a terrorist organization. They were never held to account for that. Constant, Jodel Chamblain, who was involved in the major massacre, who was implicated in the assassination of the Haitian Justice Minister, Guy Mallori, they were never brought to justice, and neither were Bush or Clinton for the backing of them. And because of this failure to enforce the murder laws, people who should be serving prison terms, are now leading an insurrection.

AMY GOODMAN: In fact, Emmanuel Constant is right here in the United States. Can you explain what happened to him when he came here and why he's protected, as Bush is talking about a war on terror, and on terrorists?

ALLAN NAIRN: Well, FRAPH was involved in hundreds, perhaps thousands, of murders of civilians. At one point, they set fire to the "Fite Solil" neighborhood of Port-au-Prince. It's an undisputed fact that they were launched by US intelligence. Clinton's Secretary of State, Warren Christopher, confirmed that fact after the initial report came out. I had several interviews with Constant and also with Colonel Collins, and the US obviously doesn't want that fact and that relationship gone into. After the US military came in and occupied Haiti, they seized the files, the archives of FRAPH, and the police, and the Haitian military, and they have kept them. And Haitian prosecutors and investigators who wanted to probe the terrorist acts by these forces haven't been able to get the access they should. And Constant has, in essence, been given a sanctuary in the United States.

AMY GOODMAN: We're talking to journalist and activist, Allan Nairn, who exposed the relationship between FRAPH, the paramilitary death squad in Haiti, during the coup of 1991 to 1994, the relationship between FRAPH and the US intelligence agencies. Also on the line with us is Congress member Maxine Waters. On the issue of Emmanuel "Toto" Constant, who is right here in the United States: Congress member Waters, is there any move in Congress, in being a part of the war on terror, to go after this person, who is responsible for so many deaths, and to call for his trial and imprisonment here in the United States?

REP. MAXINE WATERS: Unfortunately, no. He's walking around in New York. He has been sighted by several people who have mentioned having seen him, and as your guest was saying, Allan Nairn, that he was on the CIA / DIA payroll, and he's protected. I wouldn't even be surprised if he didn't end up back in Haiti, just as you have heard, that Guy Philippe is back there, and Chamblain is back there. These murderers and ex-FRAPH members re-entered without anybody saying a word. The United States knows where these guys are. They may still be on the CIA payroll, but certainly they would know what their movement is. They know that they're back. They know that they're armed, and they know what they're doing. It's a *coup-d'etat* in motion all over again with the same players. And this time, not only do you have the same players, they appear to be working in cooperation with not only our government, but the so-called opposition committee of 184 that's led by Andy Aparat.

And while Andy Aparat and the so-called Negotiators on Behalf of the Civil Society, as they call themselves, are refusing to sit down at the table and work with the so-called International Committee, and sign off on some kind of peace agreement, FRAPH, old FRAPH members just keep moving.

It's a game that's orchestrated all with [Roger] Noriega at the helm. The opposition keeps refusing. FRAPH keeps moving. The president [of Haiti] is backed up against the corner. The international players one by one will come out and say, "Well, you have to resign." All they'd have to do is send a stabilizing force. It doesn't have to be huge numbers if they wanted to pro-tect a democratically elected president who only has two years to go in his term. The agreement that he signed basically said that we would let them choose the Prime Minister, who has the responsibility over the cabinet and the police force. But that's not good enough. They want the whole thing right now. They want to get in control of government so they can control the elections.

JUAN GONZALEZ: One of the things that's been raised a lot in the media here in this country is the issue of rigged elec-tions in Haiti, that Aristide is really not exercising a legitimate power. There's an interesting piece in today's *New York Times*, op-ed piece that begins to unmask some of the allegations that in reality, that yes, there were some—there were some contest-ed senatorial seats in the last election that were criticized but that Aristide agreed to have all of those seats, those senators resign, had them resign, and was willing to hold new elections. What's your perspective of the issue of legitimacy or non-legiti-macy of the Aristide government?

REP. MAXINE WATERS: Well, you know, you hear allegations about Aristide, but nobody can put any facts to them. I asked—tell me, and I have researched, as people refer to the "failed elections." And what I found is, I believe there were eight Senate seats that were contested, and the question was whether or not there should be a runoff. Eventually, because there was so much confusion about it, Aristide did ask them to resign, and they did. Now, as I understand it, those elections took place before Aristide took office in his second election. He was not involved in that election, but he gets blamed for it. That's my understanding of it. So, it seems as if no matter what he does, it's not good enough.

Now, I have asked people to confirm for me the allegations about drug trafficking, corruption and failed elections, and still I don't have any facts, any information. Then people told me that, "Well, you know, he was involved with the gangs, and the gangs were out there beating up on people and attacking folks who were anti-Aristide. I have researched the story about a gang leader named Metier, who has supposedly, because of his death, is the source of the problem up in Gonaives where his brother is part of the thugs that had first took over Gonaives. What I discovered in my investigation was, there was this gang leader named Metier who worked for the president. And when this gang leader got out of hand and started to retaliate on people who were opposed to Aristide, Aristide had him put in jail! Because that's not what he was doing. What Aristide was doing is what many of us do in the cities, and that is we try to change the lives of these people who are in gangs. We try to get them gainful employment. We try to get them in school and try to get them in programs, things like that, and that's what he was doing.

When he got out of hand, and started to misuse the association he had with the president and his government, he had him locked up. And then his brother and others took a bulldozer and bulldozed the jail and broke him out. After he was broken out of jail, he was murdered. And then the opposition started the story that he was murdered by Aristide. And turned the brother and some of those people up in Gonaives against the president, and they now are in some ways joined with the opposition in carrying out the dirty end of it.

AMY GOODMAN: Finally, as we wrap up, Allan Nairn, as you reflect back on the period of the coup of 1991-1994 and look at what's happening today, your thoughts?

ALLAN NAIRN: Well, it's—what's happening now in a way is a tragedy that grew from crime. It's an unspeakable crime what's been done to Haiti. Long ago it was a rich country. It was stripped of its wealth by France. The US has backed terror there over the years. Haitian people were living on the brink of survival. When you're that poor, your only chance for getting out of it is to be great. You can't behave like a mere mortal, or you'll fall. You will die. And for a period in the early, late 80s, early 90s, Haitians really achieved political greatness. They put together a popular movement that brought down Baby Doc Duvalier. They thwarted designs in what they thought was a fixed election. An election, instead, that brought Aristide to power with two-thirds of the vote. They tried to push a popular platform that would raise the minimum wage and redistribute the wealth to the poor.

But, they were facing horrible pressures. Bush-1 and then Clinton, backing his criminal paramilitaries. Later, the US cutting off promised aid to Haiti. And they also faced the temptations of power. I mean, I think part of the fault for what's happening now does lie with Aristide. He accepted the World Bank-IMF plan under US pressure. He started to implement it. I think there is evidence that he has grown corrupt over the years. He did back gangs to fight his opponents, often former Lavalas allies. And that's a tragedy. He started behaving like many politicians do, like a normal political boss. And the popular movement has come to a low state. It's astonishing that these paramilitaries could come in to Heche and Gonaives and other places, and with a few hundred armed men take the cities. In the old days that could never have happened. The people would have risen up. They would have stopped it with their bare hands, with machetes and torn the paramilitaries apart. But, Aristide evidently has lost a great deal of popular support.

The larger crime, though, that helped to create this was the way that a few miles from Miami Beach, you have one of the poorest countries in the world, a place that has been stripped of its wealth where people live on less than $500 a year. That shouldn't be tolerated. There should be a massive transfer of wealth to Haiti from the rich countries that benefited from the old wealth of Haiti. And the law should be enforced. Criminals like Jodel Chamblain should be prosecuted and jailed. So should the first Bush, so should President Clinton for backing them over the years. And then maybe you can create a situation where Haitians don't have to be great to have a chance at survival, and they can make mistakes like everybody else and still lead a decent life.

AMY GOODMAN: Well, on that note, I want to thank you both very much for being with us. Allan Nairn, journalist and activist, won the George Polk award for exposing the role of the US intelligence in the formation of the paramilitary death squads in Haiti during the first coup of '91 to '94 and Congressmember Maxine Waters.

CHAPTER SEVEN

Haitian First Lady Mildred Aristide Speaks From the National Palace

Friday, February 27th, 2004

Democracy Now! aired a special show Friday afternoon on the latest from Haiti where opposition groups with ties to the US are preparing to invade the capital city of Port Au Prince. We spoke with Haitian First Lady Mildred Aristide, independent reporter Kevin Pina in Haiti, US Reps. John Conyers (D-MI) and Maxine Waters (D-CA) and attorney Michael Ratner.

AMY GOODMAN: From Pacifica Radio, this is a special report: "Haiti in Crisis." I'm Amy Goodman, host of Democracy Now! At this hour the streets of Port-au-Prince are barricaded, President Aristide and his wife, Mildred Aristide, are inside the palace. Armed gangs, paramilitaries are moving closer towards the capital of Port-au-Prince. Reports are that they have seized the town of Mirebalais, only 30 miles away, after taking the southern port of Les Cayes, Haiti's third largest city; but it is difficult to determine the accuracy of all this because there is a major disinformation that is going on. US Secretary of State Colin Powell has come very close to telling President Aristide that he should bow out as President before his term expires, February 2006. He told reporters whether or not he is able to effectively continue as President is something he will have to examine carefully in the interests of the Haitian people. The Reverend Jesse Jackson, visiting Libya, urged the United States to protect Aristide. Jackson said, "Unless something happens immediately, the President could be killed." He said, "We must not allow that to happen to that democracy. We must give the best troops to Haiti to protect the President's compound." In this hour we turn to the palace where I just got off the phone with the First Lady of Haiti, Mildred Aristide. This is the full tape of what she had to say.

MILDRED ARISTIDE: Amy, it's Mildred Aristide.

AMY GOODMAN: Hi. I thank you very much for calling. Why don't we just speak right away, and, that is, are you afraid for your life and for your husband's life?

MILDRED ARISTIDE: OK. The situation is quite critical. The thugs and the FRAPH and the military, who are heavily armed in the north, are sending messages repeatedly on the airways in Haiti, that they stand ready at any moment to storm Port-au-Prince. And here in Port-au-Prince, the population has erected—I am looking out the window—lots of barricades along the streets to prevent an attack. Security is at a heightened situation, but the President's resolve is very strong, as he indicated yesterday and through to this morning that what is important in this moment for Haiti, in terms of the future of Haiti, is to establish the stability and the political stability that Haiti has never had, and for there to be a continuity of governance from one president to the next.

AMY GOODMAN: We are just reading a report that says that the Bush administration believes that best way to avoid an armed rebel takeover in Haiti is for Aristide to resign and transfer power to his constitutional successor, this according to an unnamed senior US official. Meanwhile the Marine Corps indicates that it is preparing a possible mission to waters off the coast of Haiti. Any such deployment would be aimed at deterring a potential refugee crisis and protect the 20,000 American citizens in Haiti. Secretary of State Colin Powell signaled that direction—administration policy—in remarks Thursday night, said the US official who discussed the situation only on grounds of anonymity. So here we have for the first time, the Bush administration saying that the best way to avoid an armed rebel takeover is for President Aristide to resign. Your comment.

MILDRED ARISTIDE: I think that the position being taken by the United States and other members in the international community, that see that as an option, is completely antithetical to democracy and to constitutional democracy. It's a great tragedy. This will be the achievement of a coup, one of many in Haiti's hard and very sad history. We've had thirty-two coups. This will be the achievement of a coup. This will be the ability of a group, a small group, a relatively small group of convicted murderers, drug dealers. This will show their ability to the world that, in the face of elections, in the face of a vote of poor, black people, who voted for a president, and voted for a government, it will show their ability to override that democratic authority and be able to seize power in the nation. I think it is a truly sad day, not only for Haiti, but for the world.

AMY GOODMAN: Do you think the United States is behind this coup?

MILDRED ARISTIDE: I think that the international community has continuously failed to provide the support necessary to the democratically elected government to, in fact, to accomplish its goal of providing an improvement in the lives of Haitians. I think that it has been hiding behind this façade of: "There is some opposition to the president's policies." And by God, if it wasn't a democracy, you wouldn't hear that. And in fact, what you're hearing in Haiti and have been hearing for three years is the ability of the opposition to criticize and to say, "We hate Aristide," or "We support Aristide," "We don't agree with him here, we don't agree with him there." That's fine. That's democratic opposition, and that's what any healthy democracy should have. But what we have now is the ability of armed persons, and we must ask the question, "Where are those arms coming from?" because Haiti doesn't produce M-16s and other automatic weapons that we are seeing, slung behind the backs of these people. These are the same people who have killed over 5,000 people, who have been allowed by some force to come back to Haiti and to continue that reign of terror; and that's what it is. With the complicity of some of the sectors of the international community? I really don't know. I know that Haiti doesn't produce arms, so it's not home-grown. This is coming from somewhere.

AMY GOODMAN: The rebels are saying that it's left-over weapons from the Haitian army.

MILDRED ARISTIDE: Yeah, but the indications are, the volume has also increased, and so it's got to beyond the left-over weapons. And if you remember back in 1994, after the president returned, he was emphatic with the international community that not only must the military be disbanded, but it has to be disarmed. And if you remember, too, in '94, that was not done. And FRAPH, which was the paramilitary organiza-tion, which now stands convicted—one of the guys who is now in Cap-Haitien, Chamblain, he stands convicted *in absentia* for the murder of Guy Malary, who was the Minister of Justice in Haiti in 1993, and Antoine Izméry, and many other persons, suspected in the murder of other persons, but convicted of those two high-profile murders. And so now it is clear that it is the same group that has returned and which is bent on producing the same effect. And yet FRAPH in 1994, there was an attempt by the international community to say, "No, no. Let's try to fit them into the mold of an 'opposition' or a 'counter-balance' to Lavalas." And therein was the danger. And therein was the seed that was ready to sprout, as it has now, ten years later.

AMY GOODMAN: Louis Jodel Chamblain, who already was convicted *in absentia* has said, "Aristide has two choices: prison or execution by firing squad." Your response.

MILDRED ARISTIDE: What would you respond to

something like that? I would ask you to ask the international community, and perhaps the United States, what is their response. Is that the strategy that the world is saying is OK to deal with political dissention in today in the world? And if that is the case, then again I say that it is a sorry day for democracy in the world.

AMY GOODMAN: Louis Jodel Chamblain, the number-two man in the FRAPH. The FRAPH, launched by Emmanuel Constant, and US intelligence agencies, as was shown by the investigative journalist, Allan Nairn, in 1994 and 1995. Do you believe he is still on the US payroll?

MILDRED ARISTIDE: I don't know. I don't know and I think that would be better asked maybe from somebody in the Administration. I don't know. Just ask the question whether that is so. I don't know.

AMY GOODMAN: We're talking to the First Lady of Haiti, Mildred Aristide. She is in Port-au-Prince right now. It is Friday afternoon. There are barricades all over Port-au-Prince, and the armed forces moving in. They say they have also taken the third-largest city. What is your understanding at this point?

MILDRED ARISTIDE: I don't have information for the city of 'Cayes. I am truly not informed on that situation because I have kind of been out of pocket this morning, making lots of phone calls. So I am not sure if that is correctly being stated. I do know that there were some armed persons in 'Cayes whether they've taken over the city, I'm not sure.

AMY GOODMAN: Louis Jodel Chamblain said on Radio Metropole, "The fight in Port-au-Prince will not even last one hour. Actually, at this moment, we already have control inside the National Palace." He was then asked, "How is that? Because you do not have anybody in there." And Chamblain replied, "That is what you think. Let me tell you something. The people, who are going to help us get him, are already with him," referring, of course, to Aristide.

MILDRED ARISTIDE: Yeah, that's part of the psychological warfare that they are engaged in, to demoralize further the National Police. And, you know, this is a cruel way of proving what President Aristide has been saying for the past three years, that the police force, which is severely undermanned, severely under-resourced, under-equipped, is now facing M-16s, automatic rifles, and other kinds of heavy armaments, without being properly equipped on their end. So their ability to, in small numbers, and on top of that, using passers-by and children as sorts of human shields, as they did in Gonaives, has meant that the police force has not responded as aggressively as they could or as they should in this situation. Now these questions, I mean, Haiti is fraught with rumors, and that's in normal times, let alone in the times that we are living now where they said two weeks ago that I had left the country, that I had left with my children, and all sorts of things, and that I was not coming back, and here I am, right here in Haiti. I say this, but with a clear understanding and knowledge that, indeed, if forces, who are assisting them, or if whatever allies that they may have, do indeed intend to come to Port-au-Prince, I'm not going to be naïve enough to say that it won't happen.

What I say is that it will be an abomination, and this is an abomination of all the principles of democracy, and really must make everyone pause to wonder, what is democracy and what are we defending in the world when we allow a group of armed terrorists, armed murderers, convicted murderers, and drug dealers, to come and overrun a democratically elected government.

AMY GOODMAN: Why do you think the US has not intervened, and, until this point, are saying they're waiting for a political settlement?

MILDRED ARISTIDE: I truly don't know. I would urge you to be able to get an interview with some appropriate individuals in the international community to ask that question, because I can say, that on the Haiti side, that we have a direct and recent example in our history, a very recent example in our history. If you remember, Amy, and I know you were following events back in 1993. During the *coup d'état* in '93, in July 1993, President Aristide participated in a US-brokered agreement called the Governors Island Agreement, and under that agreement, the president was to return to Haiti in September, at the end of September 1993, and he was to name a new consensus government—new prime minister, new ministers. All of that was done in terms of the naming of the new consensus government. And that government did not have the adequate security to survive or to govern in any effective way in Haiti.

There was a steady escalation of violence in August, September, and October, making the President's return impossible, and the emergence of FRAPH the reality then. And in October, to be specific October 13, 1993, Guy Malary, who was not a member of Lavalas, but who was an honorable Haitian citizen, who agreed to partake in this consensus government as the Minister of Justice, was gunned down in front of his ministry, killed. And the person who stands convicted of his murder is none other than Louis Jodel Chamblain, who is today, attempting to do the same thing. And when the international community then asks, "political settlement" first, then security second, then you are condemning anyone who would come forward to the same fate as Mr. Malary at the hands of the same murderer.

AMY GOODMAN: Mildred Aristide, with this same man, who has been convicted of the murder of the Justice Minister, Guy Malary, so you know what he is capable of, saying Aristide has two choices: prison, or execution by firing squad, why are you both staying right now in Port-au-Prince?

MILDRED ARISTIDE: Because right now, the importance, in this moment, for Haiti is for the establishment of continuity in the democracy. It is no accident that Haiti is the poorest country economically in the Western hemisphere, and that it is a country whose 200-year history is wrought with instability, 32 coups, and always this notion, "if you don't like 'em, take 'em out!" We saw it most recently in a bloody *coup d'état* in 1991, when, after seven months, President Aristide was deposed and over 5,000 people killed. And so the importance is to say that democracy must survive. Now, if the forces who are speaking now and who have opined and said that democracy cannot go forward, and that, somehow, these thugs can be allowed to overrun the country and come into Port-au-Prince and do what they think they say they can do, that might require another analysis. But right now the analysis is that that democracy has to be saved or it is an incredible set-back for the country. Although, you know, the president has said that Haiti's past and Haiti's progress, democratic progress, slow, short, but sure and steady. The population will not sit back and it may be a question of averting the murder of thousands and thousands and thousands of Haitians. That is the type of violence which will be unleashed if this is allowed to go forward. And it is a question of what do we do, at all costs, to avert that, because the population has spoken. They will be slaughtered in great numbers if it is allowed to come to that, where the President is forced to leave, or if the President is killed.

AMY GOODMAN: What is the President doing? What are you doing? What are people doing in the streets now to protect the palace, to hold onto power?

MILDRED ARISTIDE: Well, there's a huge security presence here at the palace, and there's a huge mobilization on the streets of Port-au-Prince, where there are a lot of barricades that have been set up to stop any cars. So there are lots of barricades throughout the city that have been set up, really since the day before yesterday, and more so last night and tonight. And there are other measures that the government is looking to that has secured and augmented the security capabilities of the police. For obvious reasons I won't go into that. I'm not privy to that, but I know that those are going forward.

AMY GOODMAN: Are you and President Aristide in the palace now?

MILDRED ARISTIDE: Yes, I am right in my office, looking out the window. He's in his office.

AMY GOODMAN: Can you leave?

MILDRED ARISTIDE: Can I leave? If I chose to leave, I could leave. But I've got a lot of work to do this afternoon, so I am not leaving right now.

AMY GOODMAN: Where do you draw your strength from?

MILDRED ARISTIDE: It's from him. You know, perhaps it's because the US has no framework from which to understand a person like Jean-Bertrand Aristide. But this is a person with a mission. You know, he had this mission, as you know, and I know that you know his history. He had this mission as a Catholic priest, as a parish priest in the poorest of poor neighborhoods here in Haiti, and his mission was to uplift his parishioners. And that became expanded when he was asked to be a candidate for president.

The other day, in an interview, someone asked me if I am shocked by the level of opposition, and I say, "No, I am shocked by the depth of the commitment to Aristide that this country still has, because, notwithstanding his good will and his will to provide for the people of Haiti, he has been greatly handicapped in that ability by the embargo placed by the international community on Haiti's access to the resources that we need to increase the level of literacy, to increase the level of healthcare in this country, to increase the number of schools. Notwithstanding what we have done, with our fingers and our hands, the government has done has made great, significant efforts. In the last ten years since the restoration of democracy, the number of public high schools built in Haiti has doubled. There have been roads pierced and made in areas where there have never been roads. There have been over 50 parks built in Haiti. President Aristide has made electricity a reality for small towns which have never had electricity. The literacy campaign is working to undo or reverse a 75% illiteracy rate. With the cooperation that we have gotten from the Cuban government, we have doctors in areas of the country that have never seen the light of day of a health-care worker, let alone a doctor. We are now training over 400 doctors in schools in Cuba, and here in Haiti, thanks to that cooperation. These are the real issues that Haiti needs to confront. These are the real issues that Haitians look to when they decide who will and who will not be their leader. And this is what they will look to when there are the next free and fair elections, which must go forward in November of 2005.

AMY GOODMAN: Have you been negotiating with the United States over leaving and, if you are forced out, where you will go?

MILDRED ARISTIDE: No, and I won't answer any questions to those lines because we are maintaining the position that I said. That's not an issue right now.

AMY GOODMAN: We have heard some reports that there are a thousand Marines on the ground in Port-au-Prince. Is that true?

MILDRED ARISTIDE: On the ground? I just saw the deployment, as reported on Monday or Tuesday. There were 100 Marines that were sent to Haiti. Are there 1,000? I don't know. I don't know.

AMY GOODMAN: What about President Bush saying that they will not allow Haitian refugees into the United States?

MILDRED ARISTIDE: It's up to President Bush and the United States and to determine its policies and politics with respect to immigration policies. You know, obviously, in accord with international standards, with respect to refugees fleeing political violence, I can tell you it has begun. The number of refugees, the flight of refugees has begun. It's not a threat. It's not a warning. It's a reality. You look at the numbers, and you look at what happened during the *coup d'état*, and the steady increase in the number of refugees that were fleeing Haiti during the three years of the *coup d'état*. Before the coup began in September of 1991, there were practically no boat people leaving Haiti.

During the seven months we had achieved, and that's always been the goal of the President, for the Haitians to stay in Haiti, and work here for democracy, for the improvement of our lives, and for the betterment of the people. And that's what the situation was for seven months of the beginning of his term. Once the coup happened in September of 1991, the refugee situation spiraled and spiraled, and the risks, and the lives, and the numbers of bodies that washed ashore in Florida. You saw the images, and those images are damning, and they are fearing in the minds of all Haitians, and specifically the Haitians that are now in Florida.

And now we are faced with the threat of not only that, but with the threat of the thousands and thousands of lives that will be lost if these thugs are allowed to rule the day and say, "We have the power and we have the support to be able to move into a country where there was a democratically elected government and decide that we, a minority of armed persons, can take control."

AMY GOODMAN: We're talking to Mildred Aristide. If I could just briefly ask you how you came to be where you are today, the First Lady of Haiti, having been the Counsel for Fr. Aristide at the time.

MILDRED ARISTIDE: Right. I, along with Ira Kurzban, who is an attorney down in Florida, who is Counsel to the government, I worked with the government when it was in exile in Washington in 1993 and 1994, and then when President Aristide's government was restored, we continued our representation, and we decided to continue here on the ground in Haiti. Because I am of Haitian background, my parents are from Haiti, although I was born in the United States, I decided that I would come to Haiti and continue to work for the government, which I did through 1994 and 1995, and then President Aristide and I married about 15 days before the end of his first term, in January of 1996.

AMY GOODMAN: And you've had two girls, two children.

MILDRED ARISTIDE: Two girls.

AMY GOODMAN: And how old are they?

MILDRED ARISTIDE: Seven and five.

AMY GOODMAN: And you've sent them out of the country now?

MILDRED ARISTIDE: I did. On Tuesday night we did hear shooting near the palace, and the girls... The stress was not good for them, and so, because my parents are in the United States, I just decided to send them. So they are with them.

AMY GOODMAN: Ten years ago, perhaps fifteen years ago, do you think there would have been millions of people in the streets, and are there people in the streets now defending the palace?

MILDRED ARISTIDE: Oh, yes, there are people in the streets defending the palace. But you have to know that the arms being borne and the arms that the opposition has are quite significant, and so, you know, it's a very difficult situation, and they are preventing people from coming out, and the threats and the warnings coming on the radio are very significant. But notwithstanding that, there are people out there. There are people out there, and... It's a difficult situation.

AMY GOODMAN: What do you think could happen right now to prevent the overthrow of the Aristide government?

MILDRED ARISTIDE: You know, yesterday he spoke on CNN, and he said it could be as little as few dozen troops, a strong statement coming from the international community, an unequivocal statement, and a few dozen troops to say that this will not stand. It would only take that to begin the process of stabilizing the situation. To stop the flow of blood now, move towards this political resolution, which is a new consensus government, but as I said, who can come forward in the actual situation? No one. Allow that to go forward and move towards the reforms in the police force that we have been asking for repeatedly for the past three years. Professionalization, the better training, the better equipment, etc; and therein is the resolution to this crisis here in Haiti. I have to go.

AMY GOODMAN: And that was Mildred Aristide, the First Lady of Haiti, speaking to us from the palace in Port-au-Prince. The situation is grave. Armed gangs, paramilitaries are moving in on the capital, and we are going to turn right now to another person on the ground in the capital of Haiti, Port-au-Prince, Kevin Pina joins us. Welcome to this special on "Haiti in Crisis."

KEVIN PINA: Thank you Amy, I am here.

AMY GOODMAN: Can you tell us what is happening right now as you understand it and tell us where you are in relation to the palace where Mildred Aristide was just speaking to us from?

KEVIN PINA: Well I am about a mile and a half from the palace. And I actually thought about playing a little game on you, and attacking Mildred with all the lies that all of their opponents have attacked them with, so you could understand exactly where all these people are coming from, and how nasty they really are. They have said so many ugly, nasty things, rumors, and lies about the First Lady and the President. Especially, the press here that they call themselves free and independent. They may be free, but they are not independent at all. They are aligned with the opposition, clearly. They are in their camp. And you can tell it everyday that you listen to the news. An example is, everytime there is a Lavalas demonstration, they play music. They never give any coverage. Whenever there is an opposition demonstration, they pay themselves to run advertisements and spots on their radio stations, to extol the population against the government. And then they cover everything from A to Z, every chant, every nuance. William Randolph Hearst would blush in comparison to the kind of yellow journalism that the major radio stations in the capital Port-au-Prince are currently participating in.

Right now, people are very scared. They are very angry.

But they also remain resolute. They are very clear that they are willing to die and sacrifice their lives for this constitutional government to continue. And if it doesn't continue, believe you me, this is not over by a long shot. Haiti has a long history of coup d'etats. We know that there has been 32 over the last 100-year period during Haiti's history. We know that the first democratic transition in the history of the country occurred with the passage of power from President Aristide to Rene Preval, from Preval back to President Aristide. It's a matter of establishing democratic traditions in this country. And what is the best way to do that? By allowing an opposition that's been built by Washington and by Paris to overthrow this government?

First they attempted it by political means. When those political means didn't work, now enters FRAPH, the former paramilitary death squads trained by the CIA, the Front for Advancement and Progress in Haiti, and the former military, the guys of chief Guy Philippe who's a former CIA trained military officer in the Haitian army, the former Chief of Police, of Cape Haitian, the second largest city in Haiti. What is the best way to guarantee democratic traditions in this country? Is it to allow these former killers and murderers to enter the capital and to commit atrocities again? Or is it to stay the course and to allow Haiti to build democratic traditions? Whatever the faults his opponents have leveled against him, and a lot of it is serious, and a lot of this is involved to corporate media, who have continue to repeat a lot things that the opposition has created here and a lot of the things that the Haitian press helped to create here.

And its not a question of me making this up. I've been documenting that; that's been my work here in Haiti. I record the major radio stations every day, so I have the tapes, you know. I can show you innumerable examples of people being allowed to make unsubstantiated claims against the government, the major radio stations playing them, and the effect and the ripple that it had on Haiti. A recent example, is that Evans

Paul, one of the leaders of the opposition, and Lidia Clapeyons, another leader of the opposition within the democratic convergence, just yesterday had stated that President Aristide had resigned and already left the country, and that they were merely negotiating which country he would be allowed to return to. Right now I have a helicopter flying over me. It is a US military helicopter. Its not quite clear where its going, but there is a US military presence in Haiti right now. There are two of them, excuse me. Two US military helicopters flying directly over me. They are US Marine military helicopters. Its not quite clear where they're going, but they are here.

AMY GOODMAN: We're speaking to Kevin Pina, an independent journalist in Port-au-Prince describing the scene right now, saying, there are two US military helicopters above him. Just before speaking with Kevin Pina, we have been speaking with the First Lady of Haiti, Mildred Aristide who is inside the palace. We turn now to Congressman John Conyers who joins us from Michigan. We welcome you to this Pacifica Radio special, "Haiti in Crisis." Welcome Congressmember Conyers.

JOHN CONYERS: It's a very difficult time right now and I am glad that you are doing this kind of media service Ms. Goodman. Its something that's invaluable. I don't know of any else doing it in the world.

AMY GOODMAN: Can you tell us? First let's hear from Kevin Pina. I heard him yell for a moment. Kevin, are you still there?

KEVIN PINA: Yes. There are four US military helicopters. I can quite clearly identify them as Marine helicopters. They're circling above me right now. It's not quite clear where they are headed, but they are here and it is heavily armed. Those four military helicopters are heavily armed.

AMY GOODMAN: As Kevin describes what he is seeing on the ground in Port-au-Prince, Congressmember Conyers, can you tell use what you in Congress are being told by the Bush administration? The Congressional Black Caucus met with

Bush this week. What do you understand as happening at this point?

JOHN CONYERS: Well, we met with the President, the Secretary of State, and the Security Advisor. The whole point was that we urge that there be some kind of statement immediately coming forth from the President indicating his wanting to see a nonviolent resolution of the problem and to ask people to put away their weapons and help restore order. Then we wanted to make sure that the United States did not subscribe to the theory that we had to get a political solution before security could be sent in, which could be too late. Since maintaining peace and order would seem to need to proceed any political resolution of differences between at least some of the parties. The fact of the matter is, that there are operatives and organizations there that do not want peace, that do want violence. They do want to physically overthrow the existing government in Haiti.

AMY GOODMAN: Congressmember Conyers, as we speak to you I want to check back with Kevin Pina on the ground in Port-au-Prince. Kevin, what are you seeing right now?

KEVIN PINA: I am seeing several US Marine helicopters circling where I currently am. I'm not quite clear. I am going to go down. There five—you can hear them now passing right over top?

AMY GOODMAN: Yes.

KEVIN PINA: They're quite clearly US Marine helicopters. Its not quite clear, what's going on. I am going to descend into the palace right now.

AMY GOODMAN: And we were hearing reports today that there were something like a thousand Marines already on the ground in Port-au-Prince. But then we were told that this was a disinformation campaign, that there were some fifty that were there to protect the US embassy. What do you see?

KEVIN PINA: At that time that was true. At that time that was true. This is an entirely different ball game right now.

You can hear them, right now in the background.

AMY GOODMAN: Yes, we can hear them. This is?

KEVIN PINA: Quite certainly identify them. They are US Marine helicopters flying over above.

AMY GOODMAN: Are they going towards the National Palace?

KEVIN PINA: No. Its not quite clear where they are going at this moment, but they are here.

AMY GOODMAN: Kevin Pina on the ground in Port-au-Prince. We're speaking to Congressmember John Conyers. You have written a letter, Congressmember Conyers, to Secretary Ridge, urging him to use his authority under the provisions of Section 244 of the Immigration Nationality Act to designate the Republic of Haiti for temporary protected status. What does that mean?

KEVIN PINA: They're here.

AMY GOODMAN: Ah, lets go back to Kevin for a moment. Kevin?

KEVIN PINA: Hello?

AMY GOODMAN: Yes.

KEVIN PINA: Hello, I'm sorry. I'm sorry ask that again.

AMY GOODMAN: You just said, they are here?

KEVIN PINA: Yeah. We're watching many, many more helicopters enter Haitian airspace this moment.

JOHN CONYERS: How many more?

KEVIN PINA: I've counted four so far, I've counted four so far, but they are quite clearly doing a maneuver right now over the capital. Its not clear what is going on at this moment. I wish I could say more. I really can't.

AMY GOODMAN: Well, we'll continue?

KEVIN PINA: Until I can go down to a better vantage point, I really cannot give you more information.

AMY GOODMAN: Stay on the line with us?

KEVIN PINA: But there are crowds in the streets cheering.

AMY GOODMAN: Stay on the line with us and keep moving towards where you're trying to go and where you're trying to see more clearly what's happening. Congressmember Conyers, if you can explain what you are asking of the Secretary of the Department of Homeland Security, Tom Ridge.

JOHN CONYERS: We're trying to get our government to use every means possible to give every support to a beleaguered democratic government in the Western Hemisphere only miles from our own shore. And that is one of the ways that we can do it. Another way would be to form a humanitarian corridor, which would be bringing in much needed food, supplies, and medical equipment to the citizens of that country and they would have to be accompanied by people who would be prepared to protect and deliver that equipment. We are also trying to get the, we thought we were at an agreement with the French ambassador and the Canadian ambassador to raise the issue in the Security Council. We also have a meeting with the Secretary of the United Nations on Monday. And we're also considering massive demonstrations in front of the White House in support of 8 million people of color, who are standing helpless before gangs and thugs and drug lords and predators of every kind, while we stand idly by them. Maybe these helicopters are a prelude to a different scenario.

AMY GOODMAN: We are talking to Congressmember Conyers who has appealed among others to the Secretary of the Department of Homeland Security, Tom Ridge, to invoke, or designate the Republic of Haiti for temporary protected status. This is a Pacifica Radio special: "Haiti in Crisis." Kevin Pina, let's touch base with you again, in Port-au-Prince, observing at least four US military helicopters overhead in the capital for the first time.

KEVIN PINA: The opposition is reporting on the telephone, over the radio, that this is a contingent of US military to evacuate him from the country. However, the president just made a statement on the radio that that isn't the truth, in fact that an agreement has been reached for the crisis in Haiti.

AMY GOODMAN: Repeat that one more time so we can understand exactly who you're referring to. First you said?

KEVIN PINA: The opposition in Haiti, the democratic convergence along with the group 184, and Evans Paul who are announcing that these are helicopters that are here to evacuate the President; that he has just resigned. The President has stated that this is not the case, that an agreement to the crisis has been reached which may not involve the opposition.

AMY GOODMAN: And the President speaking from the National Palace?

KEVIN PINA: Yes. That's correct

AMY GOODMAN: Any more helicopters?

KEVIN PINA: Speaking through one of his advisors? Yes. Listen.

AMY GOODMAN: Kevin Pina speaking to us from Port-au-Prince, Haiti.

KEVIN PINA: Can you hear that?

AMY GOODMAN: We get the idea. As you were describing it. We heard the helicopters more before.

KEVIN PINA: It is very unclear, I want to be clear—it is very unclear what the situation is. There are contradictory accounts that are being told about what this means. We won't know until tomorrow, until the situation evolves clearly, exactly what this means. I can tell you, they continue to circle the capital right now. They're here. A show of force, clearly.

AMY GOODMAN: You continue to monitor what happens and let me ask Congressman Conyers, the Bush administration believes the best way to avoid an armed rebel takeover in Haiti, this according to a report just out, is for the President, Jean-Betrand Aristide, to resign and transfer power to his constitutional successor, according to an unnamed senior US official. Your response to that Congressmember Conyers. For the first time, saying at the highest levels, they want him out.

JOHN CONYERS: That was never brought up and, of

course, would have been vigorously rejected by all of the members of the caucus that were in the White House the day before yesterday. So I am shocked to read that Colin Powell had said, since we met with him, that he thought that for the best interest of the country of Haiti, that the president remove himself by resignation. Which again he and the president and Dr. Rice knew would be very strenuously objected to, because we have the simple proposition in front of us, that a democratic country cannot be idly watched—to go down in flames by critics, marauders, gangs—as if there were nothing we could or should do about it.

AMY GOODMAN: Congressman Conyers speaking to us from Michigan. Kevin Pina, independent journalist, on the ground in Port-au-Prince as this program is being broadcast.

KEVIN PINA: Amy, Amy.

AMY GOODMAN: Yes, Kevin. What are you seeing now?

KEVIN PINA: Can I tell you a scoop? The scoop is that the—it's not confirmed—but that the Venezuelan government may have offered unilateral assistance to Haitian government and that that has pressed the hand of the US government in Haiti.

JOHN CONYERS: To do what?

KEVIN PINA: The Venezuelan government may have offered unilateral assistance under the Rio Treaty and under the democratic treaty that was signed under the OAS recently, the Democratic Charter, that the Venezuelan government may have offered direct military assistance to the Haitian government and this may have forced the US hand. That is not confirmed, but I have several sources who are telling me that now.

AMY GOODMAN: And what would unilateral assistance mean?

KEVIN PINA: It would mean the landing of Venezuelan troops on Haitian soil under the provisions of the Rio Treaty and the Democratic Charter of the OAS—a fellow government asking for unilateral assistance to protect a constitutional democracy in the hemisphere.

AMY GOODMAN: Kevin Pina on the line with us. And how do you know—how do you come to believe that this is the case?

KEVIN PINA: People who are close to the Venezuelan embassy here in Haiti as well as people who are close to the Venezuelan ambassador in Washington D.C.

AMY GOODMAN: What we were hearing about Venezuela the past few days, was that it could be a place of asylum for President Aristide.

KEVIN PINA: Absolutely out of the question. President Aristide has made it very clear that he has no intention of resigning and he has made it clear that he is willing to die in his country.

AMY GOODMAN: Congressmember Conyers, can you make some sense of this? This is, if true, a surprise development.

JOHN CONYERS: Well, we know that the French had 4,000-5,000 troops nearby. That they thought that with some support, they would be willing to do what, perhaps, is going on in terms of the Venezuelan military. We had heard that Venezuela was one of the countries that felt strongly sympathetic to the preservation of a democratic form of government in Haiti and that there ought to be something that nations that support democratic processes would be able to do. And, so, it is not inconsistent with what I had been hearing.

AMY GOODMAN: We're talking with congressmember Conyers, who is one of the longest reigning congressmembers in Congress. Also part of the Congressional Black Delegation, the Congressional Black Caucus, who met with President Bush, deeply concerned about the situation in Haiti. Kevin Pina, on the line with us from Port-au-Prince, has just seen at least four US military helicopters come in and has put forward the idea, that possibily, and maybe you could explain this, because we also have Michael Ratner on the line with us, the president of the Center for Constitutional Rights, and I want him to hear what you have just laid out, Kevin Pina, to comment on this and the significance of this

MICHAEL RATNER: I actually heard Kevin and it is extraordinary news and a scoop. Remarkable. I just—I got to tell you, tears started rolling down my cheeks—if this is true, that actually someone is coming, Venezuela, to Haiti's aid. Let's see what happens now, because it does put the United States in an incredible position. Kevin is right about the Rio Treaty. What that basically allows is for a country within this hemisphere to ask for the aid of another country as well as the OAS agreement to protect democracy. That's a democracy that, of course, as everybody who now has listened to your show knows, that the US has done everything not to protect and in fact, is itself, probably, deeply involved in undermining. It is an incredible move. So the question is what will the United States do now? Will they actually try and prevent Venezuela from coming to help out a democracy and Jean-Bertrand Aristide? Will they actually begin to fight? Or are they being, maybe, put in a position where they actually have to defend that democracy, rather than let Venezuela come in and defend it. It would be hard to believe. They may just say to Venezuela, "Keep out or we'll kill ya." It remains to be seen what will happen, but it shows every contradiction of the United States' position. Here is a country with the populist leader Chavez coming to the aid of another country that is trying to be overthrown by the United States. The very country, of course, Venezuela, that a few months ago the US had a hand in trying to overthrow. An incredible act of solidarity, one that just really brings tears to my eyes.

AMY GOODMAN: Kevin Pina, have you heard anything else on the ground in Port-au-Prince?

KEVIN PINA: At this point I'm just watching these military helicopters circle. I have to get myself down to the palace. I need to ask people what is going on exactly. As I said, I cannot confirm what I said, but very, very reliable sources have indicated to me that that was the case and that is possibly why the US is now being forced to play its hand in Haiti. Because they would not like Venezuelan troops to land here, to give unilateral assistance. Remember these are the only two popular democratic governments in the hemisphere. They obviously stand in solidarity for one another. President Hugo Chavez himself has openly accused the CIA of trying to undermine his government, of trying to overthrow his democratically elected government. I believe, that from what people are telling me, that this was an act of solidarity because the same is in action in Haiti today. The ones who are the losers is Paris, is France. Because obviously they have tried to play the francophile, the francophone card here in Haiti. They have given tremendous support and back up, tremendous financial assistance to the opposition. They are the great losers if this is, indeed, the case in Haiti today.

AMY GOODMAN: We have just been joined by Congressmember Maxine Waters, who, together with Congressmember Conyers, went to the White House and met with President Bush. I don't know if she heard the latest news from Kevin Pina, who again, has not confirmed this, but does believe it might be that Venezuela said it would send in its own troops to help a nation in trouble in the hemisphere—that is Haiti. That might have forced the hand of the United States and that is why Kevin Pina is now seeing US military helicopters overhead in Port-au-Prince. Congressmember Maxine Waters, can you tell us what you understand at this point?

MAXINE WATERS: Well, I don't know about—well, I'm glad to hear it. Because I did hear the conversation where he talked about the connection between Venezuela, Haiti and Cuba. It is very, very clear to those of us who watch our government and its relationship to the small countries in this hemisphere and in the Caribbean, that this administration wishes to get rid of these leaders in these three countries who don't cry uncle, who are not puppets to our government—people who are responsible for creating popular movements. I absolutely agree and this Haiti policy—as a matter of fact, I have a discussion in a paper that I just read today that was sent to me, where Mr. [Roger] Noriega gave a speech and this is basically what he described in so many words—that these were the three countries that they were focused on in terms of their brand of democracy. So, I hope and pray that Venezuela is prepared to send some help to the national police force. I hope that is true. I do know that the United States is supposed to have some ships off the shores of Haiti there, but that is supposed to be to keep the people, Haitians, from getting up to Florida and other places. That's to put the immigrants, the, the—I'm so upset about all of this. Any how...

AMY GOODMAN: The refugees. To prevent the Haitian refugees from leaving Haiti.

MAXINE WATERS: Yes. Absolutely.

AMY GOODMAN: Well, let's check back with Kevin Pina right now—if he has learned anything else in the last minutes of this national broadcast: Pacifica's program, Haiti in crisis. Kevin, what do you know at this point?

KEVIN PINA: Hello?

AMY GOODMAN: Hi, Kevin, what do you understand at this point. Have you learned anything else?

KEVIN PINA: No. I'm still—these helicopters have just disappeared into the horizon. I have to make my way down to the national palace. I have to say goodbye. I obviously have a lot of work ahead of me to figure out what this means.

AMY GOODMAN: Well, thank you for being with us, Kevin Pina, independent journalist, reporting to us on the ground in Port-au-Prince, laying out an idea, a theory, that perhaps Venezuela had offered aid to Haiti, and that the United States—forcing the hand of the United States. Again, this has not been proven. Kevin Pina saying that the opposition was saying that the military was moving in to evacuate Aristide and the President saying that he was not going anywhere. Maxine

Waters, Congressmember from Los Angeles has just made reference to the refugees and the fact that she believed the US military moving in thousands of soldiers on the coast—in the Marines—in a mission off the coast of Haiti. Could you, Michael Ratner, who dealt very much with the refugees in Guantanamo from 1991-94 during the coup, could you reference, for a moment, what this means? Why the US is so concerned with the refugees and the significance of President Bush saying that they would not let any refugees leave Haiti? In fact, in the last 24 hours, the US has repatriated more than 500 fleeing Haitians.

MICHAEL RATNER: During the last coup, Amy, tens of thousands of refugees tried to flee Haiti. The United States from the beginning took a few in. After that, picked them up on the high seas and sent them back to Haiti without any refugee processing at all to determine if they would be killed, prosecuted or tortured when they would be sent back to Haiti. That's, of course, completely illegal, utterly illegal. You can't send someone back to their place of prosecution. The United States is obviously concerned, because what could undercut their whole coup policy in Haiti is refugees in Florida, a state that Bush has to take for the presidency. He doesn't want to see them land there. The United States is obviously willing to expend thousands of soldiers and hoods to be able to stop them and basically is willing to have people killed, really, to get Bush reelected. That's what this is about. There is no doubt about it. I think, those soldiers are not just there for that. I think they obviously know about Venezuela's starting to come in. Those soldiers are there, if it is a true rumor that we are hearing—those soldiers are there to tell Venezuela: You better not do this or you're going to have a war with the United States. Or, they are there so that basically after this coup is finally over, which is to say after Aristide is removed one way or another according to the United States' plan, the US troops will come in there and make peace, supposedly, and probably knock out some of the thugs, that they basically put in there to knock out Aristide. Those troops, I think, have more than a refugee purpose. They are probably there to intimidate Venezuela as well as to figure out what to do after the US-run coup is finished.

AMY GOODMAN: Congressmember, Maxine Waters, it seems that the Congressional Black Caucus is taking the lead on this issue. In fact, we are hearing very few number of other congressmembers addressing this. Can you talk about that?

MAXINE WATERS: Yes, we do have some other members that have been working with us like Jan Schakowsky and Mr. Delahunt, but basically, this is an issue that must be taken care of by us, because really Congress does not care about Haiti. Congress has been led for so long by the Haiti haters: Like Mr. Goss and Jesse Helms, and they have been spouting their venom for years and they use their power to malign Haiti in any way that they possibly can. Half of the members believe what they are told and they don't care enough to put time in on it to do investigation. We can't get them to hold hearings on this issue, and because of that the Black Caucus must take a lead. We must do everything that we can in order to save Haiti and save this democratically elected president.

AMY GOODMAN: Congressmember Conyers, how is the administration telling you that they will inform you about what is happening right now and are you encouraging people in this country—what are you telling, saying to people is the most effective thing to do at this point?

JOHN CONYERS: It is to write the President and bring ourselves to the White House to let him know and let the members of the Congress and Senate know that they should join with all of us that believe that democracy is in serious danger in this hemisphere and that we cannot stand idly by and watch and hope that someone else will do what is clearly our responsibility.

MAXINE WATERS: So they can fax and email and call.
JOHN CONYERS: Exactly.

MAXINE WATERS: Call Colin Powell and the President. We've got to get the voices up there letting them know that people know what is going on. We want to save this impending bloodbath. We want to stop it.

JOHN CONYERS: And, we are using this telephone number as an office for everyone who wants to be up on where we are and what we are doing. And if I may give it to you now, I will.

AMY GOODMAN: Yes. Go ahead.

JOHN CONYERS: 202-225-5126. And we want to tell people and give them an hourly report. Thank goodness for the Amy Goodmans of the world, if there are any others, in media that will bring this—the truth, eyewitness report, riveting—about how we in the Caucus and in the Congress are determined not to let these 8 million people have their government ravaged by the negative forces in that country.

AMY GOODMAN: Well, Congressmembers John Conyers as well as Maxine Waters, and Michael Ratner, president for the Center of Constitutional Rights, we want to thank you for joining us and I also want to let the stations know around the country that we will continue to keep listeners updated throughout the weekend. Check the KU updates as we continue to monitor Haiti in crisis. Produced by Jeremy Scahill. A very special thanks to Mike DiFilipo. I'm Amy Goodman. Thanks for joining us.

CHAPTER EIGHT

EXCLUSIVE BREAKING NEWS:

"I Was Kidnapped.
"Tell the Whole World
It Is a Coup."

Monday, March 1st, 2004

Multiple sources that just spoke with Haitian President Jean-Bertrand Aristide told Democracy Now! that Aristide says he was "kidnapped" and taken by force to the Central African Republic. Congressmember Maxine Waters said she received a call from Aristide at 9 a.m. EST. "He's surrounded by military. It's like he is in jail, he said. He says he was kidnapped," said Waters. She said he had been threatened by what he called US diplomats. According to Waters, the diplomats reportedly told the Haitian President that if he did not leave Haiti, paramilitary leader Guy Philippe would storm the palace and Aristide would be killed. According to Waters, Aristide was told by the US that they were withdrawing Aristide's US security.

TransAfrica founder and close Aristide family friend Randall Robinson also received a call from the Haitian President early this morning and confirmed Waters' account. Robinson said that Aristide "emphatically" denied that he had resigned. "He did not resign," he said. "He was abducted by the United States in the commission of a coup." Robinson says he spoke to Aristide on a cell phone that was smuggled to the Haitian president.

AMY GOODMAN: This is Democracy Now! I'm Amy Goodman. Congressmember Waters, can you tell us about the conversation you just had with Haitian President Jean-Bertrand Aristide?

MAXINE WATERS: I most certainly can and he's anxious for me to get the message out so people will understand. He is in the Central Republic of Africa at a place called the Palace of the Renaissance, and he's not sure if that's a house or a hotel or what it is and he is surrounded by military. It's like in jail, he said. He said that he was kidnapped; he said that he was forced to leave Haiti. He said that the American embassy sent the diplomats; he referred to them as, to his home where they was lead by Mr. Moreno. And I believe that Mr. Moreno is a deputy chief of staff at the embassy in Haiti and other diplomats, and they ordered him to leave. They said you must go NOW. He said that they said that Guy Philippe and US Marines were coming to Port-au-Prince; he will be killed, many Haitians will be killed, that they would not stop until they did what they wanted to do. He was there with his wife, Mildred, and his brother-in-law and two of his security people, and somebody from the Steel Foundation, and they're all, there's five of them that are there. They took them where—they did stop in Antigua then they stopped at a military base, then they were in the air for hours and then they arrived at this place and they were met by five ministers of government. It's a Francophone country, they speak French. And they were then taken to this place called the Palace of the Renaissance where they are being held and they are surrounded by military people. They are not free to do whatever they want to do. Then the phone clicked off after we had talked for about five—we talked maybe fifteen minutes and then the phone clicked off. But he, some of it was muffled in the beginning, at times it was clear. But one thing that was very clear and he said it over and over again, that he was kidnapped, that the coup was completed by the Americans that they forced him out. They had also disabled his American security force that he had around him for months now; they did not allow them to extend their numbers. To begin with they wanted them to bring in more people to provide security they prevented them from doing that and then they finally forced them out of the country. So that's where he is and I said to him that I would do everything I could to get the word out…that I heard it directly from him I heard it directly from his wife that they were kidnapped, they were forced to leave, they did not want to leave, their lives were threatened and the lives of many Haitians were threatened. And I said that we would be in touch with the State Department, with the President today and if at all possible we would try to get to him. We don't know whether or not he is going to be moved. We will try and find that information out today.

AMY GOODMAN: Did President Aristide say whether or not he resigned?

MAXINE WATERS: He did not resign. He said he was forced out, that the coup was completed.

AMY GOODMAN: So again to summarize, Congressmember Maxine Waters, you have just gotten off the phone with President Jean-Bertrand Aristide, who said he believes he is in the Central African Republic.

MAXINE WATERS: That's right, with French speaking officers, he's surrounded by them and he's in this place called the Palace of the Renaissance and he was forced to go there. They took him there.

AMY GOODMAN: What are you going to do right now?

MAXINE WATERS: I'm going to get to the State Department to find out what do they plan on doing with him. Do they plan on leaving him there or are they planning on taking him to another country? We are going to tell them we would like to see him. We are prepared to go where he is NOW and that we are demanding that we are able to see him and go where he is. And to negotiate what will be done with him.

AMY GOODMAN: Did he describe how he was taken out? We had heard reports in Haiti that he was taken out in handcuffs. Did he…

MAXINE WATERS: No, he did not say he was taken out in handcuffs. He simply said that they came led by Mr. Moreno followed by the Marines and they said simply "you have to go!" You have no choice, you must go and if you don't you will be killed and many Haitians will be killed. We are planning with Mr. Philippe to come into Puerto Rico. He will not be alone he will come with American military and you will not survive, you will be killed. You've got to go now!

AMY GOODMAN: How did President Aristide sound? What was the quality of his voice?

MAXINE WATERS: The quality of his voice was anxious, angry, disturbed, wanting people to know the truth.

AMY GOODMAN: Did he say why he had not made any calls since early on Sunday morning; that people had not been in touch with him for more than 36 hours. Certainly this plane was equipped with a telephone?

MAXINE WATERS: Oh, I don't think they were able to make any calls from the plane. They were only allowed to make calls once they landed. And I think the only call that they had made was to her mother who is in Florida and her brother. But they were not allowed…they had no access to telephone calls… to a telephone on the plane.

AMY GOODMAN: What is the next step…what are you going to do? What do you think the people in this country should being doing about this situation in Haiti?

MAXINE WATERS: First of all, I think the people in this country should be outraged that our government led a *coup d'etat* against a democratically elected President. They should call, write. Fax with their outrage, not only to the State Department but to all of their elected officials and to the press. We have to keep the information flying in the air so people will get it and understand what is taking place. And for those of us who are elected officials we must not only get to the President, we must demand that he is returned to claim his presidency if that is what he wants. If you can recall what happened in

Venezuela when Mr. Chavez was…they tried to force him out and they had someone step into the presidency and he had not resigned his presidency and he got it back. I did not have that conversation with President Aristide but we must meet with him and we must talk with him and be prepared to protect him.

AMY GOODMAN: Congressmember Maxine Waters I want to thank you for being with us again. Congressmember Waters has just spoken with President Aristide who she says said he was kidnapped and is now with his wife and surrounded by security in the Central African Republic.

RANDALL ROBINSON: The President called me on a cell phone that was slipped to him by someone—he has no land line out to the world and no number at which he can be reached. He is being held in a room with his wife and his sister's husband, who happened to be at the house at the time that the abduction occurred. The soldiers came into the house and ordered them to use no phones and to come immediately. They were taken at gunpoint to the airport and put on a plane. His own security detachment was taken as well and put in a separate compartment of the plane. The President was kept with his wife with the soldiers with the shades of the plane down and when he asked where he was being taken, the soldiers told him they were under orders not to tell him that. He was flown first to Antigua, which he recognized, but then he was told to put the shades down again. They were on the ground there for two hours before they took off again and landed six hours later at another location, again told to keep the shades down. At no time before they left the house and on the plane were they allowed to use a phone. Only when they landed the last time were they told that they were in the Central African Republic. Then taken to a room with a balcony. They do not know what the room is a part of, maybe a hotel, maybe some other kind of building, but it has a balcony and outside they can see that they are surrounded by soldiers. So that they have no freedom. The president asked me to tell the world that it is a coup, that they have been kidnapped. That they have been abducted. I have put in calls to members of Congress asking that they demand that the President be given an opportunity to speak, that he be given a press conference opportunity and that people be given an opportunity to reach him by phone so that they can hear directly from him how he is being treated. But the essential point is clear. He did not resign. He was taken by force from his residence in the middle of the night, forced onto a plane, and taken away without being told where he was going. He was kidnapped. There's no question about it.

AMY GOODMAN: How does he actually know, Randall Robinson, how does President Aristide know that he is in the Central African Republic?

RANDALL ROBINSON: He was told that when he arrived. As a matter of fact, there was some official reception of officials of that government at the airport when he arrived. But, you see, he still had and continues to have surrounding him American military.

AMY GOODMAN: You spoke with him and Mildred Aristide up to ten times a day in the last days before they were removed from Haiti. How did President Aristide sound when you spoke with him today?

RANDALL ROBINSON: They sounded tired and very concerned that the departure has been mistold to the world. They wanted to make certain that I did all that I could to disabuse any misled public that he had not resigned, that he had been abducted. That was very, very important to him and Mrs. Aristide explained to me the strange response to my calls on Saturday night. I had talked to her on Saturday morning and him on Friday. But when I called the house on Saturday night, the phone was answered by an unfamiliar voice who told me that the President was busy, a response that was strange, and then when I asked for Mrs. Aristide, I was told that she was busy, too. As she told me then, that even that early on, before they were taken away and before the soldiers came, they had been instructed they were not allowed to talk to anyone. And so, she said that was the reason she explained this today, a few minutes ago—why she was not able to talk to me and he was not able to talk to me when I called the house on Saturday evening.

AMY GOODMAN: Who did they say was the person that you had actually spoken to?

RANDALL ROBINSON: No, but it was not someone who worked at the house because they know my voice when they hear it and they respond to it because I call so many times. This was something new, a new person, a new voice, with a new kind of tone. That is when we began to be concerned that something was amiss.

AMY GOODMAN: I will ask you the same question I asked Congressmember Waters who also spoke with President Aristide. The issue of whether President Aristide resigned. Did he say he did or he didn't?

RANDALL ROBINSON: Emphatically not.

AMY GOODMAN: He said he did not resign?

RANDALL ROBINSON: He did not resign. He did not resign. He was kidnapped and all of the circumstances seem to support his assertion. Had he resigned, we wouldn't need blacked out windows and blocked communications and military taking him away at gunpoint. Had he resigned, he would have been happy to leave the country. He was not. He resisted. Emphatically not. He did not resign. He was abducted by the United States, a democratic, a democratically elected president, abducted by the United States in the commission of an American-induced coup. This is a frightening thing to contemplate.

AMY GOODMAN: And again, Randall Robinson, you said you spoke to President Aristide by a cell phone that was smuggled to him?

RANDALL ROBINSON: Yes, and I cannot call back because I have no number and the only way they can call out is by a cell phone because they have not been provided with any land line.

AMY GOODMAN: Did they say how long they will be staying in this place that they are, the Palace of the Renaissance, they say they believe in the Central African Republic?

RANDALL ROBINSON: They have not been told anything. I told her that last night I spoke to Senator Dodd's foreign policy person, Janice O'Connell, called me to say that she had learned from the State Department that he was being taken to the Central African Republic and she had also been told by the State Department that they had refused, that the South Africans had refused asylum. I told her that I didn't believe that that was true because the South African foreign minister—[noise] Hello?

AMY GOODMAN: Yes, Randall, Robinson, we hear you.

RANDALL ROBINSON: Because the South African foreign minister had called me—Foreign Minister Zuma—from India mid-afternoon on Sunday and she asked how I was doing and I thought I was going to be doing much better and I told her so. And I said because I'm sure that President Aristide has arrived in South Africa. She said no, he hasn't arrived here. We haven't heard anything from him. We don't know where he is and then we became really alarmed. She said there's been no request for asylum. So you see the State Department is telling an interested public, including members of the congress, that South Africa refused asylum. The State Department knows better. They know that President Aristide was not allowed to request asylum from South Africa or anybody else because he was not allowed to make any phone calls before they left Haiti, during the flight and beyond.

AMY GOODMAN: Anything else you would like to add from your conversation with President Aristide on this smuggled phone that he got hold of after many hours incommunicado and now saying he believes he is in the Central African Republic with the First Lady of Haiti, Mildred Aristide?

RANDALL ROBINSON: The phrase that he used several times and asked of me to find a way to tell the Haitian people, he said tell the world it's a coup, it's a coup, it's a coup.

CHAPTER NINE

EXCLUSIVE INTERVIEW

President
Jean-Bertrand Aristide

Monday, March 8th, 2004

At approximately 7:20 a.m. EST, Democracy Now! managed to reach exiled Haitian President Jean-Bertrand Aristide by cell phone in the Central African Republic. His comments represent the most extensive English-language interview Aristide has given since he was removed from office and his country.

Moments before the Democracy Now! interview, Aristide appeared publicly for the first time since he was forced out of Haiti in what he has called a US-backed coup. The authorities in the Central African Republic allowed Aristide to hold a news conference after a delegation of visiting US activists charged that the Haitian President was being held under lock and key like a prisoner. The delegation included one of Aristide's lawyers, Brian Concannon, as well as activists from the Haiti Support Network and the International Action Center, who acted as representatives of former US Attorney General Ramsey Clark. Shortly after they arrived in Bangui on Sunday, the delegation attempted to meet with Aristide at the palace of the Renaissance. The CAR government rebuked them.

Shortly after, the country's Foreign Minister held a press conference in Bangui. Armed men threatened journalists in the room, warning them not to record the minister's remarks. Mildred Aristide, the Haitian First lady, was brought into the room, but was not permitted to speak. The CAR foreign minister told the journalists that President Aristide would hold a news conference within 72 hours. Hours later, Aristide was allowed to address journalists.

In his interview on Democracy Now!, Aristide asserted that he is the legitimate President of Haiti and that he wants to return to the country as soon as possible. He details his last moments in Haiti, describing what he called his "kidnapping" and the *coup d'etat* against him. He responds to Vice President Dick Cheney's comment that Aristide had "worn out his welcome" in Haiti.

AMY GOODMAN: I am Amy Goodman from the radio/TV program Democracy Now! around the United States. We would like to know why you left Haiti.

PRESIDENT ARISTIDE: Thank you. First of all, I didn't leave Haiti because I wanted to leave Haiti. They forced me to leave Haiti. It was a kidnapping, which they call *coup d'etat* or [inaudible] ...forced resignation for me. It wasn't a resignation. It was a kidnapping and under the cover of *coup d'etat*.

AMY GOODMAN: It was a kidnapping under the cover of *coup d'etat*?

PRESIDENT ARISTIDE: Yes.

AMY GOODMAN: Who forced you out of the country?

PRESIDENT ARISTIDE: I saw US officials with Ambassador Foley.

Mr. Moreno, [inaudible] at the US Embassy in Haiti I saw American soldiers. I saw former soldiers who are linked to drug dealers like Guy Philippe and to killers already convicted, Chamblain. They all did the kidnapping using Haitian puppets like Guy Philippe, [inaudible], and Chamblain, already convicted, and basically, this night, I didn't see Haitians, I saw Americans.

AMY GOODMAN: So, you say that they kidnapped you from the country. Secretary of State Powell said that that is ridiculous. Donald Rumsfeld said that is nonsense. Your response?

PRESIDENT ARISTIDE: Well, I understand they try to justify what they cannot justify. Their own ambassador, Ambassador Foley said we were going to talk to the media, to the press, and I can talk to the Haitian people calling for peace like I did one night before. And unfortunately, once they put me in their car, from my residence, a couple of days later, they put me in their planes full with military, because they already had all of the control of the Haitian airport in Port-au-Prince. And during the night, they surrounded my house, and the National Palace, and we had some of them in the streets. I don't know how many are—were there. So it's clearly something they planned and they did. Now, if someone wants to justify what I think they cannot justify and that's—my goal is to tell the truth. This is what now I'm telling you—the truth.

AMY GOODMAN: President Aristide, did you resign the Presidency?

PRESIDENT ARISTIDE: No, I did not resign. I exchanged words through conversations, we exchanged notes. I gave a written note before I went to the press at the time. And instead of taking me where they said they were taking me in front of the Haitian press, the foreign press, to talk to the people, to explain what is going on, to call for peace. They used that note as a letter of resignation, and I say, they are lying.

AMY GOODMAN: When you went into the car from your house, did you understand you were going to the airport and being flown out?

PRESIDENT ARISTIDE: Not at all. Because this is not what they told me. This was our best way to avoid bloodshed. We talked with them somehow in a nice, diplomatic way to avoid bloodshed, we played the best we could in a respectful way, in a legal and diplomatic way. Because they told me that they were going to have bloodshed. Thousands of people were going to be killed, including myself. As I said, it was not for me, because I never cared about me, my life, my security. First of all, I care about the security and lives of other people. I was elected to protect the life of every single citizen. So, that night I did my best to avoid bloodshed and when they took me, putting me in their plane, that was their plan. My strategy was then all I could [do] to avoid bloodshed.

AMY GOODMAN: Are you being held in the Central African Republic against your will?

PRESIDENT ARISTIDE: Actually, against my will, exactly. Let me tell you, this past twenty hours on the American plane with American soldiers, including nineteen American agents who had an agreement with the Haitian government to provide security to us. They were also in that plane, maybe, to keep the truth in the plane, instead of having one of them telling the truth out of the plane. Because one of them had a baby, one year and a half in the plane—he was an American guy—and they wouldn't give him a chance to get out of the plane with the baby. My wife, the First Lady, who was born in the United States, her father and mother were Haitians, with me. She didn't have the right to even move the shade and look out through the windows. Which means, they violated their own law. Until twenty minutes before I arrived here, I didn't know where they requested to land, which means clearly, clear violation of international law. Unfortunately, they did that, but fortunately, I pay tribute to the government of Central Africa for the way they welcomed us. It was gracious, human, good, and until now, this is the kind of relationship which we are developing together. I thank them for that once again.

AMY GOODMAN: What do you want to happen now?

PRESIDENT ARISTIDE: I always call for peace. Those who realize their kidnapping cannot bring peace to the violence in my country. CARICOM, which means all of the heads of the Caribbean countries, call for peace and restoration of Constitutional order. In some way we heard the voice of Americans—American senators, American members, US members, members of the US parliament. They're all—they're all US citizens and the Haitians are actually calling for peace for the restoration of constitutional order. This is what I also call for. Allow me to give you a very simple example. Peace means for us, in this time, education and investment in health care. In my country, after 200 years of independence—we are the first black independent country in the world—but we still have only 1.5 Haitian doctors for every 11,000 Haitians. We created a university, we founded a university with the faculty of medicine that has 247 students. Once US soldiers arrived in Haiti after the kidnapping, what did they do? They closed the faculty of medicine and they are now in the classrooms. This is what they call peace. This is the opposite of peace. Peace means investing in human beings, investing in health care, respect for human rights, not violations for human rights, no violations for the rights of those who voted for an elected president, and this is what it means. It means that, for humans in the world, today this is their day, [inaudible] men in the world, all together, we can all work hard to restore peace and constitutional order to Haiti.

AMY GOODMAN: This is President Jean-Bertrand Aristide speaking from the Central African Republic. Did you want to return as President to Haiti now?

PRESIDENT ARISTIDE: If it's possible now, yes, now. Whenever it's possible, I am ready because this is what my people voted for.

AMY GOODMAN: Are you being held—do you see yourself as being held as a prisoner in the Central African Republic?

PRESIDENT ARISTIDE: Here I say it again, the people and government and the President, President Bozize, they are gracious, the way they treat us. I just paid public tribute to them, and if you have citizens of Central Africa listening to me, allow me to tell them [inaudible], which means thank you very much, because their country is a country called zo-quo-zu, in the language which means every human being is a human being. All that is to say, we, I, am grateful to them. But when you living in a house or in a palace that is their palace, which is a good sign of respect for us, and we are living in their conditions, although it's still good because of the way they welcome us, we also feel that we should be in Haiti with the Haitian people doing our best to keep investing in education, health care, building a state of law. Slowly, but surely, building up that state of law.

AMY GOODMAN: President Aristide, at least five people were killed in Haiti on Sunday. Opposition leaders say it was pro-Aristide forces that opened fire. Also including journalists—a Spanish journalist based in New York was shot dead. Another was also shot. Your response?

PRESIDENT ARISTIDE: First of all, I wasn't there, and I don't have many pieces of this information to comment, but the respect that I have for the truth, I will make some comments but I say it again, I wasn't there. I don't have yet any information so, I cannot go too far in my way to analyze the situation. I do believe because for the past years, each time drug dealers like Guy Philippe, people already convicted like Chamblain kill people, we heard exactly what I just heard. They blame the non-violent people and they blame the poor. When are poor, they are violated in their eyes, like the way they did. When you are already convicted, you are not violating human rights. So, I think or I suspect they are lying when they talk like that, accusing my followers.

AMY GOODMAN: What message do you think the United States is sending the people of Haiti and the rest of the world in their actions with you?

PRESIDENT ARISTIDE: I think the citizens of the United States supporting democracy in Haiti, the Haitian people, and Haitians in Washington, Brooklyn and Milano, in Boston and elsewhere, calling for my return to Haiti and the constitutional order, I think all the citizens of the United States [inaudible] are a sending a very strong, critical signal to all of the countries in the world willing to work in a peaceful way for democracy. But those who [inaudible] me are sending a very wrong signal because if we don't reach the result of democratic elections and then we cannot be elected and then you do that here and elsewhere, the signal you are sending is "No to democracy," while you are talking about democracy. So, that's why I wish they would connect—they did realize that they are wrong and they have a new approach, which will be protecting the rights of humans in the world. Because in the world, what do we mean, meaning peace. What do we mean, meaning democracy. What do we mean, we need to invest in human beings. Therefore, to go back, we should not send wrong signals as they did.

They went to Iraq. We see how is the situation in Iraq. They went to Haiti. We see how is the situation in Haiti. Pretending they are imposing democracy with people killing people. Why don't they change their approach to let democracy and the constitutional order flourish slowly, but surely. After imposing a criminal embargo on us being, from the cultural point of view, very rich from a historic point of view very rich but from an economic point of view, very poor because we are the poorest country in the western hemisphere, after imposing their economic embargo upon us, because the people wanted one man, one vote, so equality among us.

Then they use drug dealers, they use people who are already convicted, pretending to lead the rebellion, while they went to Haiti killing people in Gonaives, killing people in Cap-Hatien and killing people in Port-au-Prince and elsewhere. And now they continue in the face of the entire world, blessing impunity supporting those killers. My god, I have said it's really ugly that image they project in the face of the world. Now it's time for them to change, to respect them but we will also respect the truth. That's why respectfully, we are telling them the truth. I said, when someone is wrong, the wrong way to behave is to continue to be wrong. The right way to behave is a move from wrong to being right. Now, it's time to move from being wrong on their side to become right by supporting the constitutional order.

AMY GOODMAN: President Aristide, Vice President Dick Cheney said you wore out your welcome in Haiti. It's time for you to go. He also said—can I get your response to that?

PRESIDENT ARISTIDE: How can someone, after the kind of elections they had, now talk like that regarding Haiti where you had fair, democratic elections regarding the elected president. I think someone can have power, but that does not mean, we cannot see the truth and say the truth. I respect the rights of every single citizen in the world to talk, and we have to be tolerant because this is also about democracy. That's why I have respect for him, I respect the way, his way to talk, but at the same time I have respect for my people and for the truth. I say it, and I say it again, the Haitian people are a non-violent people. They voted for democracy. They will continue to fight in a peaceful way for democracy, and I will continue to be faithful to them doing the same. The peaceful approach, fighting peacefully for the restoration of the constitutional order.

AMY GOODMAN: Do you still consider yourself President of Haiti?

PRESIDENT ARISTIDE: Yes, because the people voted for me. They are still fighting in a peaceful way for their elected president. I cannot betray them. That's why I do my best to respect their will.

AMY GOODMAN: Well, how would you describe the situation in Haiti today? US and French forces and Canadian troops are in Haiti. It is something you called for before you left, to support you, and to protect the—and to protect you there, then?

PRESIDENT ARISTIDE: Yes, I called for them before they forced me to leave the country. Now, unfortunately, they are in Haiti. They don't have the elected president with them to move with the constitutional order. But despite of that, I wish the United Nations in Haiti through peacekeepers can help keeping peace in the country, protecting all the Haitians, every single Haitian, because the life of every single man or woman is sacred. You have to respect that. So, I wish they will protect the lives and the rights of every single citizen by the time we continue to work hard, peacefully to restore democracy in Haiti.

AMY GOODMAN: Vice President Cheney said, "I have dealt with Aristide before when I was Secretary of Defense. We had a crisis involving Haiti. He left of his own free will. He signed a resignation letter on his way out. He left with his security detail on an aircraft we provided, not a military aircraft, but civilian charter. Now, I suppose he's trying to revise history. But the fact of matter was, he'd worn out his welcome with the Haitian people. He was democratically elected, but he never governed as a democrat. He was corrupt, and he was in charge of many of the thugs that were committing crimes in Port-au-Prince. The suggestion that somehow the United States arrested him or forcibly put him on an aircraft to get him to leave, that's simply not true. I'm happy he's gone. I think the Haitian people are better off for it. I think now they'll have an opportunity to elect a new government, and that's as it should be."

PRESIDENT ARISTIDE: Well, as I said before, he has the right to talk, and I respect his right, as I have the right to say the truth, and I will be saying the truth. I disagree with him, and I will continue to believe that the Haitian people will continue to fight in a peaceful way to restore democracy, and when the day will come to have elections, of course, they will have the ability to vote. Unfortunately, they didn't want a *coup d'etat*, and they never wanted the Haitian people to keep moving from election to election.

They preferred the Haitian people to move from *coup d'etat*, to *coup d'etat*. We celebrated 200 years of independence. We had a [inaudible] *coup d'etat*. We know, usually, who can choose to be behind the *coup d'etat*. So, now that we just had a kidnapping which they call a resignation, which others call *coup d'etat*, it's clear that some people will be do their best to justify, but they may not be able to justify, and I will continue to be on the side of the truth, on the side of the human rights, on the side of all of those who knew about what happened, and stand firm with the Haitian people. The heads of the Caribbean countries stand firm for the restoration of the constitutional order, for peace. We have senators in the United States, members of the US House, citizens in the States standing firm for peace, for democracy, for constitutional order, and I join them.

AMY GOODMAN: Why do you think that the United States government does not want you to be the President of Haiti?

PRESIDENT ARISTIDE: Maybe, if you could see just one single example, it can tell the world a lot. I know I have already told you that, but I will go through it again. In 200 years of independence, making Haiti the first black independent country of the world, we still have 1.5 Haitian doctors for each 11,000 Haitians. Then we have a university who the faculty of medicine had 237 students. [inaudible], they are now in that faculty of medicine, they closed it. And the students are out, and this is not what they decided to do. If, have a government or a president willing to invest in health care, apparently they don't want that. If you have a president or government willing to invest in education, maybe they don't want that. I will continue to believe that we must invest in human beings. We must invest in education and health care. This is what will bring peace. Because peace is not an empty word. It has to be full. Investing in education and health care, bring the real peace to the country, and what they call peace is not the real peace. It is violence. It is kidnapping. What we call peace through education is telling the world that we are right.

AMY GOODMAN: President Aristide in your news conference, did you say that your country is now in the midst of an unacceptable occupation?

PRESIDENT ARISTIDE: It's an occupation, and the

last example I just gave says it is an occupation. How you can imagine that you come to me, you want to be in peace, and you close my university and you send out 247 students of medicine in the country where you don't have hospitals and you don't have enough doctors. God, this is an occupation. When you protect killers, when you protect drug dealers like Guy Philippe, like Chamblain, when you protect the citizens of the United States in violating the law of the United States, Mr. Andy Apaid is a citizen of the United States, violating the Neutral Act, the way with this act will destroying our democracy, and once we do that, then this is an occupation.

AMY GOODMAN: Is it true that—did you say that your security force around—that protected you in Haiti, from the Steele Foundation—that they were told by the US government they could not send in reinforcements?

PRESIDENT ARISTIDE: Yes. As a matter of fact they blocked them, to stop providing security, and 25 guards did come the day after, they were prevented to come. So it was a clear strategy to move their way according to their plan. Now, time is gone. Unfortunately I need to stop because they just asked me to leave.

AMY GOODMAN: Do you think that you will ever see Haiti again as President?

PRESIDENT ARISTIDE: I will. I will once the Haitian people and the international community continue to work hard. It's not impossible.

AMY GOODMAN: What do you think people can do in the United States?

PRESIDENT ARISTIDE: I think they can continue to mobilize human resources to help bring peace for Haiti—democracy for Haiti. This is what the Haitian people want: Peace and democracy.

AMY GOODMAN: Will you be leaving the Central African Republic? Do you want to leave?

PRESIDENT ARISTIDE: No, no, no, no. They are not

asking me to leave the country, they are asking me to end the...

AMY GOODMAN: I understand. I understand. I understand, but do you want to leave the country? Do you want to return immediately to Haiti?

PRESIDENT ARISTIDE: If I can go today, I would go today. If it's tomorrow, tomorrow. Whenever time comes, I will say yes, because my people, they elected me.

AMY GOODMAN: What is stopping you from returning today?

PRESIDENT ARISTIDE: Because it means to clear the way, and that's what we are doing now.

AMY GOODMAN: Thank you very much for joining us, President Aristide.

PRESIDENT ARISTIDE: Thank you so much for you and wishing that we can meet again in Haiti.

CHAPTER 10

IN-DEPTH

The Full Story of Aristide's Kidnapping

Thursday, March 11th, 2004

J ust back from the Central African Republic, Kim Ives, an editor of the Haitian newspaper *Haiti-Progres*, discusses the events surrounding President Aristide's overthrow. Ives spoke with Aristide in his native Creole and was able to piece together what is probably the most comprehensive picture of what Aristide says happened to him and his wife the morning they were forced out of Haiti.

A delegation of activists, journalists and lawyers from the US has just returned from the Central African Republic where they held a series of meetings with Haitian President Jean-Bertrand Aristide. In fact, it was their presence in the CAR that ultimately forced the authorities there to allow Aristide to appear publicly and hold a press conference. Earlier this week, Democracy Now! did an extensive interview with Aristide, the most extensive English-language interview since his removal from Haiti.

The delegation that returned to the US last night is holding a press conference today at the National Press Club. The group includes one of Aristide's lawyers, Brian Concannon, as well as representatives of the Haiti Support Network and the International Action Center, who went to the CAR representing former US Attorney General Ramsey Clark. Kim Ives was also on the delegation. He is the Editor of the newspaper, Haiti-Progres. He had a chance to speak with Aristide in the Central African Republic in Aristide's native Creole and was able to piece together what is probably the most comprehensive picture of what Aristide says happened to him and his wife the morning they were forced out of Haiti.

•   Kim Ives, editor of the Haitian newspaper, Haiti Progres.

AMY GOODMAN: Kim Ives joins us in the studio right now, an editor of *Haiti-Progres*. Welcome to Democracy Now!

KIM IVES: Thank you, Amy, Juan.

AMY GOODMAN: Can you tell us what President Aristide told you and how it differs from what we have heard?

KIM IVES: I think the reports we've heard and, I think, the definitive account was in the *Washington Post*, was that the US intervened around 4:00 or 5:00 a.m. When Lewis Moreno, the US Deputy Chief at the US embassy came by—

JUAN GONZALEZ: 4:00 or 5:00 a.m. On what day?

KIM IVES: On the 29th. That is Sunday morning. As if he just came in to basically respond to Aristide's call to get him out of there. Well, the *Washington Post* report is good in the respect that it makes clear there was a quid pro quo playing for a signature on a supposed resignation letter. It really minimizes the US role. What President Aristide explained to us was that the US pressure really began 12 hours earlier. For half a day, he was locked in a battle with pressure, phone calls, and diplomats and military that had surrounded his home. They had come in and, as has been reported, the Steel Foundation, which was the unit—the company which has provided his close security, was essentially dismissed by the US armed forces, their former employers. They were taken by helicopter to the airport while Aristide was told that if he did not resign and cede power, he would be left defenseless and would be killed.

JUAN GONZALEZ: To just go back—it is to get the facts, given all the confusion around this. In other words, on Saturday, his security were told—were dismissed and he was left without security on Saturday evening before the events that the government claims happened?

KIM IVES: Yes. That is the essence of the gun that was put to his head. They removed the security in the face of this band of "rebels" which is most assuredly US financed, headed by Guy Philippe, former US Special Forces-trained Police Chief—trained in Ecuador under their guidance, and Jodal Chamblain, the CIA supported death squad leader. We see that they were essentially saying: if you don't cede to our demands, we will let these people come and kill you and, in addition, thousands of Haitians in Port-au-Prince. They were essentially saying, they would unleash this rebel force on the city. Now how much damage this rebel force could have done is not a question because they're not that big and the people had really dug in their heels. But, nonetheless, Aristide apparently felt enough pressure that he felt he had to bow to these demands.

JUAN GONZALEZ: Now when he left his home, sometime around Sunday morning around 4:00 or 5:00 a.m., what happened then?

KIM IVES: Then he was taken in a cortege of US military cars and with Moreno. He was taken to the airport.

AMY GOODMAN: Moreno being?

KIM IVES: The deputy chief of the US Embassy.

JUAN GONZALEZ: Who has been in Haiti a long time. I remember him back in 1990-91, when he was actually the one who was certifying which Haitians could get political refugee status in the United States.

KIM IVES: Right. He was part of the vetting program of what was, in essence, an Operation Phoenix in Haiti.

JUAN GONZALEZ: And he's had a long history. I interviewed him. He was in Peru during the time of the shining path, he was in El Salvador. He's been in a lot of hot spots around the world as a State Department employee.

KIM IVES: Right. He is a real technician of the empire. I think the essence was that the embassies of both the US and France had asked Aristide, or had, I think, even drafted from one of the accounts that—from somebody else's who spoke to Aristide told me—that they, in fact, drafted a resignation for him, which he refused to sign and that was a lot of the struggle during the night. In the end result, he drafted his own letter, which was couched and had a conditional clause in it and, to him, provided him the wiggle room to say that he had not, in fact, resigned, which is really a moot point because it's clear it was forced no matter what you say. So, this was—since he was taken to the airport, he found his Steel Foundation core there and they were put on the plane. It was interesting. He explained to us that they felt it necessary to take these 19 Steel Foundation employees, including the one-year-old child of one of them, one of the soldiers had had—one of the security guards had had a child with a Haitian woman, they took them all to Africa because, according to Aristide, they feared that one of them might leak the news about their kidnapping. And so they took them all to Africa and then flew them back to the United States, which was an interesting—

AMY GOODMAN: Kim Ives, I was struck in your written description of what Aristide told you. You said that when he left his home that night, that he expected that he was going to a press conference?

KIM IVES: Right. That was part of it. It was tricky. Foley, James Foley, the US Ambassador, had told him he would have an opportunity to address the international and Haitian press and, furthermore, that his home would not be looted. First, he did not get a chance to address the press. He was just bundled directly onto the plane. And secondly, almost immediately after he left, his home was looted and it was after it was looted that they posted a guard. So, this shows you—and not only his home was looted, but the Aristide Foundation, which houses a medical school, was also looted. And this was in the Democracy Now! interview. I think he talked about that, too. This is now where they are housing the soldiers of the US In this medical school in a country which has 1.5 doctors per 11,000.

AMY GOODMAN: Kim Ives is our guest. He is an editor at *Haiti-Progres* newspaper, a Haitian weekly. If you can describe what happened when you got to the Central African Republic.

KIM IVES: Well, we went direct to the gate of the palace, because we couldn't get through on the phones. This is part of the thing you have to understand. First, it takes two days to get to this country. You have to take several airlines and we got the one direct flight a week from Paris and even that is an ordeal. And, when we got there, we found a phone system, which is intermittent at best. This is all part of the isolation they put him in. They got him ensconced in the palace, supposedly for security. So, you have this ring of security around him. So we finally decided, well, let's go to the palace, even though we knew it was a long shot.

First of all, to approach the palace, you can't even drive along the wall to it. You have to approach it down the street, driving about three blocks. I guess, so they can determine whether or not to fire on you. We got up to the gate and were met there, of course, by armed guards. The guy came out and said, well, I have to check if you can meet. He went in and came back out and said, no, the defense—the minister said no meetings on Sunday. And I said what minister? And he said, defense minister. I don't know why he was calling a defense minister for a meeting with Aristide. And then we had proceeded to say, well, can Aristide come out and meet us? No. Can we send him a note? No. Can we leave him a telephone number to call us? No. So absolutely no contact with him was allowed. We went back to the hotel and then we learned, from other press who had been there, that this had caused a real brouhaha in the palace, that they had hastily called a press conference where they brought Mildred Aristide, President Aristide's wife, out and even this was quite a comedy because they had told the press when they got there, there would be no pictures, no video, and no recording. The press by and large left. They had to call them back. Then they said OK, we'll allow a recording.

AMY GOODMAN: Is it true that armed men came in and told all the photographers and video people to close their machines?

KIM IVES: That is correct. And, in essence, they stalked off in protest. Finally, the press conference went forward and Mildred Aristide was posed a question by the Reuters correspondent and she said, "well, I take my leave from the Foreign Minister." In essence, asking him if she could respond and he just stared at her. She stared at him and there was no answer given. They persisted and they said does she have the right to speak? Can she talk? And eventually the Foreign Minister said no. We had a number of meetings with him and it was clear he did not view Aristide in a favorable light. That he was accepting the US version that this was a fallen dictator, etc. This press conference went over like a lead balloon. So, then they had to hold another the next day and that's where Aristide spoke. But even this press conference was, we could say, very constrained. Aristide spoke in French.

AMY GOODMAN: And this is the one that could be filmed.

KIM IVES: That one was filmed. The press was there in force. But immediately after he spoke in French, CNN said could you give the version in English, just so nothing is lost in translation, and he did. And immediately after that, the Foreign Minister intervened to say, I'm sorry, but there will be no more questions in English. So, he was essentially making the conditions of interview. Perhaps it was that they wanted to follow exactly what was being said or perhaps they wanted to limit its effect. But that was the essence of the press conference and they curtailed it to only about four or five questions after that.

JUAN GONZALEZ: Now when you got to speak with Aristide directly, you mentioned in the article—the statement you've written—the events leading up to the coup, and why it was particularly on this weekend, the 28th and the 29th that all of these events unfolded because the American public has large-ly been told that the US government moved in to assist, to pre-vent a massacre or a chaos in Haiti. What are some of the events that have not come to light that you were able to glean from your discussions with President Aristide?

KIM IVES: Well, one of the things that Aristide told us was that, for him, one of the reasons they had to move that night, that Saturday night, was because the South Africans had sent a planeload of rifles and ammunition to support the police, who were basically outgunned by the rebel, "rebel" forces. We have to remember the rebel forces had new M-16s and armor-piercing ordinance, etc. And so the planeload was due to arrive Sunday. Furthermore, there was talk that the Venezuelans were going to send help. While we weren't able to go into it, into the question of the Venezuelans with Aristide—and I should say that our discussions with him were somewhat constrained because a lieutenant colonel from the Communications Ministry was sitting right across the table from us as we spoke. So, although we spoke in Creole in an effort to circumvent his eavesdropping, it was still—there is enough common words in Creole and French to make that a little difficult.

AMY GOODMAN: Would you have been able to speak quietly in English the whole time?

KIM IVES: Hard to know. I think they might have spo-ken English. That was our assumption. So, we chose Creole to continue the discussions.

JUAN GONZALEZ: You also mentioned that there was some US congressmembers that is were due to come down to the country as well.

KIM IVES: Yes. Maxine Waters had tried mightly to join the delegation. In the end, it wasn't possible and we had to real-ly scramble. I have to say it was a real ordeal trying to get this over there and we had real trouble from every logistical point of view in turning this out.

AMY GOODMAN: It is quite astounding to look at—listen to the comments of the Bush Administration officials. One of them, along the way, was that when he stopped—and was it Antigua as they were refueling, not knowing where they were going, ending up in the Central African Republic?—he was able to speak with CARICOM leaders, now a statement has come out of the CARICOM community, 15 countries in the Caribbean, condemning the kidnapping, the ouster, and calling for a full investigation. Then they said that he had been denied amnesty, this is front page *New York Times*, had been denied political exile, political exile in South Africa. So, that night I went over to meet the South African ambassador to the United Nations and asked why they had or if, in fact, they have had denied him South African sanctuary and he said, no, he never applied and now we see this delegation coming.

KIM IVES: Right. And there is delegation coming. I think it's difficult—a delicate problem for him because on the one hand, he doesn't want to look for political asylum. He wants to go back immediately to Haiti and asking for political asylum as an acknowledgement that you will be out of the country for a while, on the one hand. And two, I think he recognizes the difficult political situation that a country like South Africa is facing. They took a lot of heat for the support in standing by Haiti during the bicentennial celebrations and there is an electoral season in South Africa. So, he's quite aware that these dynamics are taking place. And I think that it is making some sort of consideration of that. So, I—the same is true for Central African Republic. He has not made a request for political asylum there. And so he is in some sort of limbo in this respect.

AMY GOODMAN: Has Aristide—did he directly say to you I'm being held prisoner

KIM IVES: No, he did not. On the contrary. He had to keep insisting he was not being held prisoner, but the facts speak for themselves. You can see the difficulty just to get there, to phone there, to see him. The manifest hostility, or I should say, disapproval, of the Central African authorities, at least the ones we were dealing with primarily and the Foreign Ministry. Central Africa is itself a very—it's a coalition government of sorts that came into power through a coup itself—is in not at high state of stability and—

AMY GOODMAN: Dire poverty, also very dependent on the United States and France.

KIM IVES: Exactly.

AMY GOODMAN: Interesting how Iraq was a US-British led force. This is a US-French led operation. In fact, didn't Aristide say he holds the French ambassador to Haiti as well responsible for his kidnapping and wants to bring charges?

KIM IVES: Yes. The French were involved in all this pressure and, in fact, were in some ways leading the charge. And I think he also explained to us how he arrived in the Central African Republic was, a call—the official version is that the plane was in the air and nobody wanted him and they were looking for some place and the Central African Republic was the only place.

AMY GOODMAN: Voyage of the damned?

KIM IVES: Right. The reality was that some arrangements were made through Gabon, and President Bongo of Gabon, which is the leader of the Central African States—thats sort of the dean of those states. And so Bongo called the Central African Republic and said, essentially, listen, you're going to take Aristide. This is what the foreign minister explained to us. So, this was done through the US, France, Gabon talking. No Haitian officials were involved. Nobody from Haiti was involved. This was a purely US-French operation.

JUAN GONZALEZ: And, of course, France probably more than the United States had more to lose from Aristide continuing in the presidency since he was beginning to lay claim to reparations from France for the period of colonialism and slavery.

KIM IVES: This is precisely it. You had the restitution for

$21.7 billion, which was on the table, and we saw a lot of rivalries were put aside to get Aristide out—between the ruling groups in Haiti or the comprador bourgeoisie and the big land owners, who generally are constantly squabbling throughout Haitian history for power. They put aside their differences to get together, which we see from Andy Apaid representing the bourgeoisie and Guy Philippe and Jodel Chamblain. And, we saw the France and the US who have also been sort of vying, pushing aside their differences. So you saw this union, unity, come between rivals against Aristide because he represented the people and because he was a representative of the popular will in Haiti.

AMY GOODMAN: How do you account for the thousands of people who came out—the news reports were in support of the ouster of Aristide, calling for him to be returned so he could be tried?

KIM IVES: I always put into—I take with a huge grain of salt the reports I get from Haiti because when I've been there I've seen how they'll transform a crowd of a couple of hundred into thousands.

AMY GOODMAN: Jodel Chamblain signing autographs and Guy Philippe being held up.

KIM IVES: Exactly. This has been, unfortunately, a lot of mainstream press takes their leaded from the opposition press in Haiti, which is owned by the Haitian bourgeoisie, 70% to 90%. And, hence, the vision they give is often completely skewed and completely erroneous. Meanwhile, you'll have massive demonstrations, a million people almost on February 7 out in support of Aristide. You don't see a picture. You don't hear words about that. So it's a real—you have to take the reporting we get from Haiti with a real grain of salt.

JUAN GONZALEZ: It's always—I generally look at where was the staging place for the demonstration? If it started in Haitianville, then you know that it represented the upper classes of Haiti.

KIM IVES: Right.

AMY GOODMAN: I saw an interesting report, I don't know if it was an AP or Reuters wire report. Deep down, many paragraphs down, where it is always most interesting to look, usually at the end of a piece, was a quote of a pro-Aristide supporter. When asked why the pro-Aristide forces weren't out last weekend, he said because the US forces are protecting the anti-Aristide forces and we're afraid.

KIM IVES: Right. And that is the thing. They're constantly blaming the victim, putting the victims as the aggressors and vice versa.

AMY GOODMAN: The records of Jodel Chamblain. We've gone through it before, but very briefly, because the mainstream media so rarely mentions just who these coup leaders are. Just very briefly, Louis Jodel Chamblain, and Guy Philippe, John Tatoune who led the insurrection and then the new prime minister, LaTortue.

KIM IVES: Jodel Chamblain was the number two of the FRAPH death squad created at the suggestion of the CIA, funded by the CIA, responsible in large measure for the—for a majority of the 5,000 killed and disappeared in Haiti during the 1991 to 1994 *coup d'etat*. Guy Philippe, US-trained police chief. He had been a soldier, was taken to Ecuador during the coup where he was trained by US Special Forces, was brought back with a group of 11 others. They were called the Ecuadorians. They were by and large police chiefs. They attempted a coup under the Preval administration. It was discovered, which is again proof that this just isn't about Aristide, it is about democracy. They were taken to the Dominican Republic despite repeated extradition requests. He was never returned. He's also been accused of drug dealing in Panama and Ecuador. John Tatoune came up from the underclass of Gonaives and was also a FRAPH head involved in the 1994 Raboteau massacre. Again, here is a guy who you heard so many press reports about, Omnio Mitane is a terrible chieftain of violence and yet

Tatoune, he's presented as almost a hero.

AMY GOODMAN: We only have a minute. But the Prime Minister now being brought—a chosen Prime Minister, LaTortue, brought from Florida, among the first things he is said to have to restore: the Haitian military.

KIM IVES: Right. And this was the former Foreign Minister of Leslie Manica of a neo-Devaluerist sector. He is some sort of neo-Devaluerist technician. I think, we can expect him to work hand and glove with the US And, he was Leslie Manica, just to remind listeners, was the president who was installed by the military in 1998 after the election massacre of 1987.

AMY GOODMAN: Well, I want to thank you very much for being with us, Kim Ives, an editor of *Haiti-Progres*, just came back from the Central African Republic where he met with Aristide and spoke with him in his native Creole. Today at noon and the National Press Club, he and the delegation who went are holding a press conference. This is Democracy Now!.

CHAPTER ELEVEN

Democracy Now!'s Exclusive Updates

Aristide Returns to the Caribbean

On Saturday night (March 13) shortly before 9 p.m.* a US and Jamaican delegation left Miami headed to the Central African Republic to return President Jean-Bertrand Aristide and his wife Mildred back to the Caribbean.

Aboard the plane were US Congresswoman Maxine Waters, TransAfrica founder Randall Robinson, attorney Ira Kurzban, and Jamaican parliamentarian Sharon Hay-Webster will be representing the government of Jamaica and CARI-COM. Accompanying the delegation are journalists Amy Goodman of Democracy Now! and Peter Eisner of the *Washington Post*.

Leaving for the Central African Republic

AMY GOODMAN: We have just gotten on the plane which will take us to the Central African Republic. We've been told we have two stops, one in Saint Thomas and one in Dakar, Senegal. When we arrived at the private airport, security guards said the delegation that is headed to pick up President Aristide and his wife would not be allowed to hold a news conference, that they did not have permission for that and after some back and forth, the delegation decided it would walk off the airport property to hold their news conference because press was here to ask why they are going and to get the update on the situation

---

*All times EST.

with President Aristide. They [the security guards] agreed that they'd be able to hold the news conference on the property of the airport.

And so now we are inside the plane. Everyone has just sat down. We've been told what the itinerary is and we are ready to go. I have to go. The plane is about to take off on this historic mission to bring back the democratically elected president of Haiti, Jean-Bertrand Aristide, and his wife, Haitian-American Mildred Aristide. Reporting on the tarmac in Miami, I am Amy Goodman for Pacifica Radio's Democracy Now!.

In the Central African Republic

At around 4 p.m. on Sunday, Goodman filed her first report from Bangui, Central African Republic:

AMY GOODMAN: I'm standing in front of the Presidential Palace where two guards are at the doors. President Aristide, US Congressmember Maxine Waters and the representative of CARICOM of the Jamaican Prime Minister, PJ Patterson, are meeting with the president of the Central African Republic. This we believe, just before the delegation will leave. At this point it looks like the delegation will go back tonight with Aristide and his wife Mildred Aristide returning them to the Caribbean, they'll be going to Jamaica for the next weeks. When President Aristide first saw the US delegation, he came out and said he was very happy to see them, very sad to know that those in Haiti are suffering so much, so he said today he has mixed feelings. I'm Amy Goodman reporting from Bangui, Central African Republic where just an hour or two ago the US delegation landed that was coming to retrieve President Jean-Bertrand Aristide and his wife, Mildred Aristide, and return them to the Caribbean, to Jamaica where they will spend the next number of weeks. The US delegation was led by Congressmember Maxine Waters and Randall Robinson coming from St. Kitts—founder of TransAfrica. Also, representative of Prime Minister P. J. Patterson of Jamaica—representative of CARICOM—came with a letter to present to the President of the Central African Republic saying that the delegation is now taking President Aristide and thanking the Central African Republic for its hospitality. President Aristide has made it very clear in his interview with Democracy Now! that he says he was kidnapped and that this is a *coup d'etat* backed by the United States. Today we met with his security here who was taken on the plane with him, we'll have more on that story later. But he reiterated in a blow-by-blow description exactly what happened on that late night, early morning of February 29th, 2004 when US diplomats came to President Aristide's home and, he said, told them that he was taking them to a press conference. They loaded into a car, instead were taken to the airport with a US jet with an American flag on it. A number of US military piled in, changing their military uniforms into civilian-wear, wearing baseball caps. The security of the Aristide administration also piled in apparently having been told in advance that the Aristides were being taken to the airport and they were flown off like this to Antigua not knowing where they were headed. President Aristide and Mildred Aristide are being kept in a wing of the presidential palace. It is well guarded, there are soldiers around, they are in a side wing of the palace and they are not free to come and go and it is clear that they very much want to return to the Caribbean, unclear where they will end up after Jamaica. Again, President Aristide and Mildred Aristide now about to leave the Central African Republic, we believe within the next hour or so. The delegation will take them back to Jamaica. We made our way from Miami to St. Thomas to Dakar, Senegal and then landed in Bangui and we believe we'll be taking the same route back so I'll be filing reports. Reporting from Bangui, Central African Republic, I'm Amy Goodman for Democracy Now!.

Shortly after Goodman filed that report, a major drama began to unfold in Bangui. There was a several-hour-long stand-off that raised serious questions about whether the Haitian leader would be permitted to leave Africa. The events also suggest that the US or other foreign governments may have attempted to prevent or delay Aristide from leaving.

Throughout Sunday, there were a flurry of meetings between Aristide and the President of the Central African Republic, Gen. Francois Bozize. Some of the meetings also included Rep. Maxine Waters and Jamaica's emissary, Sharon Hay-Webster. As the stand-off was beginning, Goodman filed this report:

AMY GOODMAN: I'm Amy Goodman, reporting from Bangui, Central African Republic at the Presidential Palace. It is a stand-off right now. A negotiation that is taking place between the President of the Central African Republic and the US delegation that wants to take President Aristide and his wife Mildred back to the Caribbean tonight. As Ira Kurzban, the attorney for President Aristide puts it, is Aristide a prisoner or not? Is he free to go or not? That is the decision that the President of the Central African Republic will make in the next hour.

Representatives of the delegation, the Representative of CARICOM, of Jamaican prime minister P. J. Patterson, Sharon Hay-Webster, US Congressmember Maxine Waters, and John-Bertrand Aristide met with the President of the Central African Republic just about 20 minutes ago. And he will get back to them with his decision, he says, in the next hour or so. And certainly the United States and France are very much working behind the scenes. The delegation in the United States negotiating with the State Department. Congressmember Maxine Waters, who heads this delegation, going back and forth with the State Department. They said they have no stake in this. Although as I reported earlier, the very interesting testimony of the security chief of President Aristide here, France Gabriel, who described what happened on February 29 in the wee hours when the US diplomats Moreno came to President Aristide's home. Gabrielle says, as President Aristide has said, that he was told he was taking him to a press conference. Instead, they were taken to the airport. This is a remote place, the Central African Republic, extremely difficult to get to, a plane going out about once a week. He has been kept from a lot of questions and exposure. President Aristide—now he wants to leave. In Jamaica, his two daughters, five and seven years old, the Aristides have never been apart from their children for this length of time.

At that point, the satellite phone went dead. Twenty minutes after Goodman filed that report, Aristide emerged from his meetings in the Presidential Palace and Amy once again called in:

AMY GOODMAN: President Aristide told Democracy Now!, he said he thinks the President must consult with those who called him before Aristide arrived here. The United States, France, and Gabon, to decide whether they should let him go. We're going right now into the Presidential Palace. I will call you back.

Forty minutes later, Goodman filed an update on the stand-off:

AMY GOODMAN: I'm Amy Goodman reporting from the Presidential Palace in Bangui, Central African Republic where [inaudible] has just met with the President of the Central African Republic, Francois Bozize, along with the Aristides. This followed a private meeting that the two presidents had and it looks like the delegation is headed home tonight with the Aristides, headed back on a 17-hour flight to the Caribbean to deliver the Aristides to Jamaica, where they will reunite with their two daughters, aged seven and five. At the gathering, at the meeting of the, at the meeting with the President of the Central African Republic, he presented the Aristides with two gifts. One, a picture made of thousands of butterfly wings and another made of the rare woods of this area. The entire US delegation was there, yet led by Congressmember Maxine Waters, the pilots are sleeping aboard the chartered flight, waiting for word about whether the delegation will be allowed to take Aristide. It looks like the word is yes. The President of Haiti is returning to the Caribbean. I'm Amy Goodman, reporting for Democracy Now!.

Moments later, just after 1:00 a.m. Central African time, Goodman called in with breaking news:

AMY GOODMAN: The chief of protocol here in the Central African Republic has just confirmed that we're headed to the airport. The Aristides are going to Jamaica. Mildred Aristide told Democracy Now! she is very much looking forward to reuniting with her two small daughters, Christine and Mikael. I'm Amy Goodman in Bangui.

Right before the delegation headed for the airport in Bangui, Goodman got reaction from delegation members Maxine Waters, Sharon Hay-Webster and Randall Robinson:

AMY GOODMAN: We're at the Presidential Palace in Bangui, Central African Republic. It is confirmed that the US delegation is taking President Aristide and his wife, Mildred Aristide, back to the Caribbean. The person who headed this delegation is US Congressmember Maxine Waters. Maxine Waters, your comment on this historic night.

MAXINE WATERS: Well, it has been quite an experience. We're here at the capital in Bangui and we are on our way to the airport with President Aristide and his wife Mildred Aristide. It's been a long day. We've had an opportunity to meet with the President [inaudible]. They have treated him very well. They were kind to us. We had an opportunity to learn a [inaudible]. We are bringing with us President Aristide and his wife Mildred, where they will be received in Jamaica. It has been a long day. It has been an interesting day. We've learned a lot about the Central African Republic and we are very pleased to be getting on the airplane and he will be in Jamaica by tomorrow.

AMY GOODMAN: I'll now bring you Sharon Hay-Webster, the CARICOM representative, Jamaican Parliamentarian, who delivered a letter to the President of the Central African Republic, Francois Bozize.

SHARON HAY-WEBSTER: Hello. I can say that on behalf of the team, all of us who were here to represent President Aristide and CARICOM, all of this family, within the diaspora of the US and the Caribbean, we're happy to have our family members here in Africa and to have a positive decision to be taken and for him to be returned to his family within CARICOM. [Inaudible] to be reunited with his children and now the family will plan together and how they will proceed from here.

AMY GOODMAN: That is Sharon Hay-Webster, Jamaican Parliamentarian. We're also joined by Randall Robinson, who is one of the members of the US delegation. He is founder of TransAfrica, an author that came from St. Kitts for this trip. Your thoughts today as we head to the airport.

RANDALL ROBINSON: I'm very pleased that President and Mrs. Aristide are going to be reunited with their children tomorrow in Jamaica. It's refreshing. I'm extremely relieved. They have been our dear friends for so long and to see them joining us, going home now, is a great joy and a great relief.

Moments before the Aristides and the delegation left for

the airport, the Director General of State Protocol of the Central African Republic, Stanislas Moussa-Kembe, told Goodman, who at the time was inside the Presidential Palace in Bangui, that the Aristides would be allowed to leave the Central African Republic immediately. He told Goodman, "You're headed to the airport."

Just before they boarded the plane in Bangui, Goodman managed to speak briefly with the Haitian President:

JEAN-BERTRAND ARISTIDE: I will say that because they were so gracious in welcoming us here, it's natural that while we are leaving, the first thing we say is thank you, and in the old language, which is Sangho, thank you very much is [says thank you in Sangho].

AMY GOODMAN: President Aristide, can we have your thoughts on your return to the Caribbean?

JEAN-BERTRAND ARISTIDE: In the Caribbean family, we find the African Diaspora, too. Now that we are in Africa, moving towards Jamaica, we are moving from one big family to the same family somehow. That's why we will continue to do our best to promote peace, friendship, for all of us as members of the same family as brothers and sisters.

AMY GOODMAN: We are headed to the airport right now, so we can't talk anymore, but we will be providing you further reports. President Aristide and Mildred Aristide, along with the US delegation are on the airport road. The charter jet is being prepared, and we are going to be there in just a minute, taking off from the Central African Republic at around one in the morning, it will be a seventeen-hour flight stopping in Dakar, Senegal, and St. Thomas, the Virgin Islands, and perhaps other places, and finally making it to Jamaica.

Leaving the Republic

Once on board the plane, Goodman phoned in one last report:

AMY GOODMAN: We're on the plane. Everyone is on board. We begin our 17-hour flight. We will head to Dakar, Senegal and then to Cape Verde, possibly to Barbados and finally, we will wind up in Jamaica, where the Aristides will reunite with their family to a reception by the Jamaican Prime Minister P. J. Patterson. The whole US delegation is on board. I'm Amy Goodman reporting from the tarmac in Bangui, Central African Republic for Democracy Now!.

Despite the historic significance of this trip, with Aristide defying the warnings of the Bush administration and returning to within 200 miles of his native Haiti, this has not been a major story in the corporate media. In fact, Democracy Now! contacted CNN in an effort to get them to cover the story. A CNN producer told us, "We're going to stand down on this one." While most corporate media outlets are virtually ignoring this story, it is very much news in Haiti and in the Caribbean and it is certainly being monitored very closely in Washington. The Jamaican government is bracing for the arrival of the Aristides. They're deploying a large security operation. Aristide has not relinquished his office as President of Haiti, despite what the Bush administration is saying. The violence continues in Haiti. The US military is there and has shot about a half dozen Haitians in the last week or so.

The last report she filed before Monday's broadcast was at 4:30 a.m. EST. She was in Cape Verde, an island nation off the coast of West Africa, the last stop before they began crossing the Atlantic Ocean. This is Goodman's report filed from the tarmac at the airport in Cape Verde, Africa:

AMY GOODMAN: I'm Amy Goodman reporting from Cape Verde, where we've touched down for just a minute for the final refueling to cross the Atlantic Ocean. President

Aristide and his wife, Mildred Aristide, for these first six hours of the trip, looking ahead to returning to the Caribbean, to Jamaica, to see their two daughters, meeting with the Prime Minister of Jamaica, P. J. Patterson. The US delegation on board is extremely excited at being able to accomplish their mission of picking President Aristide up from the Central African Republic. On the plane, I spoke with President Aristide and Mildred Aristide about the situation in Haiti. They talked about their concern over a number of issues, among them, that the University of Peace has been made the US military base in Port-au-Prince. The hospital there, the medical school that teaches Haitians to become doctors, the teachers have been threatened, and are afraid to work there. This in a country of total destitution that has one of the lowest rates of doctors in the world. Mildred Aristide also talked about the looting of her home. As soon as the Aristides left, their house was robbed. Contrast this to what happened after the first coup, when the US government promised the coup leader, Raul Cedras, his home would be protected, and they actually paid him two thousand dollars a month for the use of it. The plane is packed, the delegation is—our next stop, we believe will be Barbados many hours from now, and then we'll be moving on to Jamaica.

CHAPTER TWELVE

Pressuring Jamaica

Sunday, March 14th, 2004

Democracy Now! co-host Juan Gonzalez interviews Hazel Ross-Robinson, adviser to President Jean-Bertrand Aristide and wife of delegation member Randall Robinson:

JUAN GONZALEZ: For perspective on the latest developments, we go now to the Caribbean to St. Kitts. We're joined on the telephone by the wife of Randall Robinson who, of course, is with the Aristides on the plane over the Atlantic. Hazel Ross-Robinson is also a close friend of the Aristides. She is an adviser to the Haitian President. Welcome to Democracy Now!.

HAZEL ROSS-ROBINSON: Thank you for having me.

JUAN GONZALEZ: Well, your reaction to the—everything that's happen in the past 48 hours.

HAZEL ROSS-ROBINSON: Well, I am very relieved that the Aristides are on their way back to the region, back to family as CARICOM's representative described it and, most importantly, back to their children. I am, however, saddened that once again the positive strides being taken by Jamaica and CARICOM, in defense of fairness, in defense of justice, in the name of Caribbean unity, in the name of dignity throughout the African Diaspora, I am saddened that the US media have decided to completely ignore that. Thank heavens, however, for Democracy Now! because through your efforts, you are making sure that those people who are interested in these types of issues are made aware of the extraordinary stand in defense of what is right, that have been taken by Prime Minister Patterson, CARICOM, Congresswoman Maxine Waters, my husband, and others who are trying to keep the spirit and the hope of the Haitian revolution alive.

JUAN GONZALEZ: Do you have any sense of what kind of pressure was put on the Jamaican government over this issue by the Bush administration?

HAZEL ROSS-ROBINSON: Well, from my discussions throughout the region, it is clear that there has been enormous pressure placed on these little countries to reject President Aristide, Mrs. Aristide, and their family. It is very important to the powers that be that President Aristide, twice elected by the people of Haiti, and the voice for Haiti's poor, it is very important to the powers that be that he be seen as an isolated and rejected figure. Of course, nothing is farther from the truth. And as you can see, he is back today in the family of the Caribbean. Now we all know that Secretary Powell, National Security Adviser Rice and Secretary of Defense Rumsfeld have all said publicly how much they oppose his return to the region. So, we can only imagine the kind of pressure to which these small and precious democracies in the Caribbean have been put and they are to be praised for their adherence to principle. They're not being anti-American. They are not trying to challenge the United States. Indeed, they're trying to embrace those principles on which the United States was supposed to be built. Fairness, justice, democracy, decency, and human compassion. Today is an extraordinarily positive day for the Caribbean. I'm very proud of CARICOM and very proud of P. J. Patterson.

JUAN GONZALEZ: Now the Bush administration has claimed that they intervened in the situation in Haiti to prevent further bloodshed. But obviously bloodshed has continued since the US troops moved in. Could you talk a little bit about what you know about that?

HAZEL ROSS-ROBINSON: Well, I have been talking to some people inside of Haiti and just as took place between 1991 and 1994, when President Aristide was ousted by the combined forces of the Haitian economic elite and Haitian military, the same unions that ousted him again this time with the help of the United States and France, of course. In talking to Lavalas supporters, supporters of the President, two things are happening. First of all, as we can expect, many of them have gone on underground because they are really quite afraid, so many of them have gone into hiding. Surprisingly, though, we have only seen on the very occasional coverage that we now get from the mainstream media, we have seen that thousands of Haitians, pro-democracy Haitians, pro-government Haitians continue to go on the street demonstrating and protesting the fact that their President was not allowed to complete his term. Most troubling are reports that Haitians in the poor areas are being murdered. They're being massacred. That is rather troubling. I have also been told that those Haitians who have dreadlocks seem to have been singled out. As you may have seen on a recent CNN telecast, that there were a number of bodies with dreadlocks. At that time, I did not realize they were part of some sort of extermination campaign, but my colleagues in Haiti tell us that Haitians with dreadlocks have definitely been targeted. In addition to that, I am told that the US Marines and the other international forces that are there are completely brought into the talk about Aristide's supporters, or the government supporters being shamares, and the word used over and over to demonize President Aristide's supporters, the government's supporters. So there is panic. There have been many deaths, as you know, and there is a terrible sense of injustice and sadness because ten years of hard work to help to bring the Haitian people forward, despite the rise of vicious embargo imposed by France, Canada, and the United States, ten years of hard work seem to have been, at least temporarily, swept aside by the "liberators" who came across from the Dominican Republic and by their powerful allies in France and in the United States.

JUAN GONZALEZ: And finally, I'd like to ask Hazel Ross-Robinson, do you still hold out hopes that President Aristide will be able to be returned to power?

HAZEL ROSS-ROBINSON: That is something that only President Aristide and the people of Haiti would be able to decide. I think that that is something that I'm simply not equipped to respond to. But what I can say, though, is that it was very important to the people of Haiti and to black people throughout the Diaspora because of the history of Haiti and because of the glory of the Haitian revolution. It was so important to all of us that President Aristide, or whoever the elected President was at this time, be allowed to complete his term. Symbolically and psychologically that was important, and we feel rather betrayed that once again the powerful nations of the earth have manipulated circumstances in such a way that once more Haiti and its people are seen as objects of ridicule, objects of pity. It didn't have to be this way. It has been a terrible betrayal and I find it quite heart breaking.

JUAN GONZALEZ: Well, thank you very much, Hazel Ross Robinson. Her husband, Randall Robinson, is on the plane with President Aristide, returning to the Caribbean, to Jamaica, along with Democracy Now!'s Amy Goodman. We've been providing you with exclusive coverage of that return trip on today's show.

CHAPTER THIRTEEN

Defying Washington, Haiti's Aristide Arrives in Jamaica

Monday, March 15th, 2004

** *BREAKING NEWS* **

DEMOCRACY NOW! BROADCAST EXCLUSIVE

Kingston, JAMAICA (March 15)—Democracy Now! host Amy Goodman reports that Haitian President Jean-Bertrand Aristide has arrived in the Caribbean nation of Jamaica. Moments after his plane touched down at Norman Manley International Airport at approximately 2:20 p.m. EST, Aristide and his wife, Mildred, were escorted to a helicopter, which transported them to an undisclosed location on the island nation.

The Jamaican emissary that traveled with the Aristides from the Central African Republic to Jamaica, Sharon Hay-Webster, told Goodman that the Aristides were headed to a government compound on the country's north coast. Hay-Webster said she could not disclose the exact location for security reasons. Aristide made no public statements at the airport.

Amy Goodman has been traveling with Aristide, his Haitian-American wife, Mildred, and the delegation of US and Jamaican officials that accompanied the Aristides to Jamaica, which has offered to temporarily host them. Goodman is one of only two journalists that traveled with the Aristides.

In returning to the Caribbean, Aristide is defying the Bush administration, which has stated clearly it does not want Aristide in the Western Hemisphere. Meanwhile, the US-installed "prime minister" of Haiti said today he was recalling

Haiti's ambassador to Jamaica and putting relations on hold over Aristide's return to the region.

The US has also criticized Jamaica for offering to host Aristide. "Jamaican authorities are certainly taking on a risk and a responsibility," said James Foley, the US Ambassador to Haiti. "His coming within 150 miles from Haiti is promoting violence."

"Ambassador Foley's responses are unfortunate," Jamaican emissary Hay-Webster told Democracy Now!.

She said: "[Jamaican] Prime Minister Patterson, as chairman of CARICOM, took that position not as a personal consideration but as a response to a request by President Aristide and also in conjunction with speaking to his other colleagues in the Caribbean—that is the prime ministers and presidents of the other nations within the Caribbean. This is not a singular decision from Jamaica. This is decision by CARICOM. Is the ambassador threatening all of CARICOM? He may have a lot of surprises ahead."

A LONG JOURNEY 'HOME' TO THE CARIBBEAN

Since the Aristides left the Central African Republic, Goodman traveled with them and the US-Jamaican delegation on the chartered Gulfstream jet that ultimately returned Aristide to the Caribbean.

Shortly before the delegation arrived in the Caribbean, Goodman reported the following:

"The US delegation on board is extremely excited at being able to accomplish their mission of picking President Aristide up from the Central African Republic. On the plane, I spoke with President Aristide and Mildred Aristide about the situation in Haiti. They talked about their concern over a number of issues, among them, that the University of Peace has been made the US military base in Port-au-Prince. The hospital there, the medical school that teaches Haitians to become doctors, the teachers have been threatened, and are afraid to work there. This in a country of total destitution that has one of the lowest rates of doctors in the world."

Preceding Aristide's departure from the Central African Republic, there was a several-hour-long stand-off in the capital, Bangui, that raised serious questions about whether the Haitian leader would be permitted to leave Africa. The events also suggest that the US or other foreign governments may have attempted to prevent or delay Aristide from leaving. Aristide, who was democratically elected, has charged that he was "kidnapped" from Haiti on February 29 in a US-orchestrated coup. Aristide reiterated these allegations in a series of interviews with Goodman in Bangui and on-board the plane.

Throughout Sunday, there was a flurry of meetings between Aristide and the president of the Central African Republic, Gen. Francois Bozize. Some of the meetings also included Rep. Maxine Waters (D-CA) and Jamaican parliamentarian Sharon Hay-Webster, who is representing Jamaica's Prime Minister P. J. Patterson, as well as the Caribbean Community (CARICOM). At one point, Aristide emerged from a meeting with Gen. Bozize inside the presidential palace. Amy Goodman reported that when he came out of the meeting, Aristide was "surrounded by military."

After the initial round of talks with Bozize, Aristide spoke briefly with Goodman. She reported that "Aristide thinks that President Bozize must consult with those who called Bozize before Aristide was taken to the CAR—the US, France and Gabon—to decide whether Bozize should allow Aristide to leave the country." These were the three countries that orchestrated Aristide's stay in the CAR.

It is not yet clear what possible role the US and other foreign governments played in the stand-off that preceded Aristide's departure from the CAR. In an interview with Goodman as the stand-off was underway, Aristide's lawyer Ira

Kurzban questioned whether the Haitian president was being held prisoner because he was not being allowed to leave when he wanted.

Ultimately, after numerous meetings, the group was told they would be allowed to leave the CAR. Moments before they took off, Goodman conducted a brief, exclusive interview with Aristide. "Because they [the government of the CAR] were so gracious in welcoming us here, it is natural that while we are leaving the first thing we say is thank you," Aristide told Goodman.

She then asked Aristide for his thoughts on his impending return to the Caribbean. "In the Caribbean family, we find the African Diaspora too," said Aristide. "Now that we are in Africa, moving toward Jamaica, we are moving from one big family to the same family somehow. That's why we will continue to do our best to promote peace, friendship for all of us as members of the same family, as brothers and sisters."

Mildred Aristide told Goodman she is very much looking forward to reuniting with her two small daughters.

The delegation that traveled to the CAR to escort Aristide back to the Caribbean was led by Rep. Waters. "It has been quite an experience," Waters told Goodman just before they boarded the plane in Bangui. "It has been a long day... We are very pleased to be getting on the airplane and he will be in Jamaica by tomorrow."

Sharon Hay-Webster, the emissary of Jamaica and CARICOM, told Goodman, "I can say that on behalf of the team, all of us who were here to represent President Aristide and CARICOM, all of his family within the Diaspora of the US and the Caribbean, we are happy to meet with our family members here in Africa and to have a positive decision to be taken—that is for him to be returned to his family within CARICOM... and for him to be reunited with his children and all the family to plan together as to how they will proceed from here."

TransAfrica founder Randall Robinson, who is a close friend of the Aristides, is also a member of the delegation. "I am very pleased that President and Mrs. Aristide will be reunited with the children tomorrow in Jamaica," Robinson told Democracy Now!. "It is refreshing. I am extremely relieved. They have been out here for so long. To see them joining us, going home is a great joy and a great relief."

Before the Aristides departed Bangui, President Bozize presented them with two gifts—one a picture made of hundreds of butterfly wings, the other a piece of art made from rare wood from the CAR.

US OPPOSED ARISTIDE'S RETURN TO CARIBBEAN

Throughout Sunday, Goodman reported on the stand-off in the CAR over the fate of Aristide and his wife Mildred. She indicated that there was some question among the visiting delegation on what role Washington was playing in the situation. What is clear is that US officials have declared very publicly that they do not want Aristide to return to the Western Hemisphere.

"We think it's a bad idea," National Security Adviser Condoleezza Rice told NBC's "Meet the Press." "We believe that President Aristide, in a sense, forfeited his ability to lead his people, because he did not govern democratically."

Defense Secretary Donald Rumsfeld, on CNN's "Late Edition," said: "The hope is that he will not come back into the hemisphere and complicate [the] situation."

In Haiti, the chairman of the US Joint Chiefs of Staff, General Richard Myers, said, "As far as Aristide's return to the region is concerned, if that increases the violence here, then that would be extremely unhelpful."

Jamaican Prime Minister Patterson, speaking as current chairman of the 15-nation CARICOM, has called for an international investigation into the circumstances of Aristide's removal from Haiti February 29. The 53-nation African Union echoed that call last week.

CHAPTER FOURTEEN

Exclusive:

Aristide's Bodyguard Describes the US Role In His Ouster

Tuesday, March 16th, 2004

In a broadcast exclusive, Democracy Now! interviews Aristide's bodyguard Franz Gabriel on what transpired the night of February 28-29 when President Aristide says he was kidnapped by the US and removed from Haiti.

AMY GOODMAN: I had a chance to speak with a person who witnessed firsthand the events of that night. He is Franz Gabriel, Aristide's personal bodyguard and security aide. I spoke with him in a wing of the Presidential Palace near where the Aristides were being held and where they were meeting with the delegation that came to escort them back to the Caribbean. Gabriel provided further details on the role of the United States in Arisitide's removal, in particular the role of the deputy chief of mission at the US Embassy in Haiti, Luis Moreno. Peter Eisner of the *Washington Post* was also in the room. During the interview, Gabriel's mobile telephone rang many times. I began by asking Franz Gabriel to describe his last night in Haiti.

FRANZ GABRIEL: Well I was at the house at 5:00 a.m., when I saw some US personnel from the Embassy, of which I recognized Mr. Moreno. They came in to tell the President that they were going to organize a press conference at the embassy, and told him to be ready to accompany them. The President called Mildred, and we boarded the vehicles to go to the Embassy, we rode to the Embassy. As we were heading towards the Embassy, passing the airport, we ended up making a right inside the airport, and that's when I realized that we were not going to the Embassy.

PETER EISNER: [inaudible] also thought he was going to a press conference at the embassy?

FRANZ GABRIEL: Yes. That's what Mr. Moreno had invited him to do. And as we were at end of the runway threshold, we saw a plane pull in, and just parked there. And then we saw some military personnel.

AMY GOODMAN: What was the press conference supposed to be about?

FRANZ GABRIEL: The press conference was probably going to be about his leaving of power.

AMY GOODMAN: Whether he would leave power?

FRANZ GABRIEL: Whether he would leave power, yes.

AMY GOODMAN: So what happened when you saw the plane, what happened next?

FRANZ GABRIEL: Well, I saw deployment of US Marines everywhere. And that's when I realized that, you know, it was something serious. I saw a white plane with a US flag at the tail of the aircraft, and it looked strange because it was no markings on it. And as the plane stopped, they had us board—everybody boarded the plane. And all the Steele Foundation agents that were in contract with the government to give the President security, boarded the plane also.

AMY GOODMAN: Are you with the Steele Foundation?

FRANZ GABRIEL: No, I'm not with Steele, I was with President Aristide. And they all boarded the plane. They sat us down and didn't tell us where we were going. And then they closed the door. Didn't even want us to pull the shades up. We just sat there and waited. They started down and then we just—they close up the gate of the plane, and then we took off.

AMY GOODMAN: Did you know where you were going?

FRANZ GABRIEL: No, we never knew where we were going.

AMY GOODMAN: And how long—

FRANZ GABRIEL: When we landed in Antigua, this is what they told us, we landed in Antigua. And in Antigua, we—they told us that there is a possibility that we might be going to South Africa. But the person that was relating the information, was relating it to one of the Steele Foundation agents. And I overheard it when he said it. As we were sitting down, they started take our names down. And they asked the Steele Foundation people where, you know, where they were going.

PETER EISNER: Who is "they?"

FRANZ GABRIEL: The guys that were part of the coup on the airplane.

PETER EISNER: They didn't identify themselves?

FRANZ GABRIEL: Well, they boarded the plane dressed as military. As soon as they boarded the plane, they changed clothes. They were, you know, they had baseball hats and regular civilian clothes. They no longer appeared as military.

AMY GOODMAN: And they were who? Who were these people that changed their clothes?

FRANZ GABRIEL: Well, they boarded the plane. You know, they were dressed in full military gear.

AMY GOODMAN: US military?

FRANZ GABRIEL: US military.

AMY GOODMAN: And so you left Antigua, overhearing that you might be going to South Africa, but not knowing.

FRANZ GABRIEL: Yes, I left Antigua thinking that we might be going to South Africa because that's what they said. As we were on the plane, we landed in an island called Asuncion Island, and that's when they told us that South Africa would not accept us, and that they didn't know where we were going because they didn't have a country that would accept us. So, therefore…

AMY GOODMAN: Had the President applied to these countries?

FRANZ GABRIEL: The President didn't even know where he was going...

You are listening to Franz Gabriel, President Aristide's personal bodyguard. Peter Eisner of the *Washington Post*—the only other journalist on the plane with the delegation—asked Gabriel whether President Aristide agreed to resign the night of his departure from Haiti. He asked about reports that Aristide handed a resignation letter to the deputy chief of mission at the US Embassy in Haiti, Luis Moreno. Gabriel says he saw no such exchange and that it didn't happen in front of him. Aristide has maintained that he did write a message in Creole that the US says was his letter of resignation but that it was mistranslated in English to make it appear as if he resigned.

AMY GOODMAN: The President calls it a kidnapping. Do you agree with him?

FRANZ GABRIEL: I would say so. I would say that it is a kidnapping.

AMY GOODMAN: Do you have—you talked about the US presence at the airport taking him to the airport. What were the other evidences of US involvement?

FRANZ GABRIEL: Well, a plane that shows up at quarter to six in the morning, out of nowhere, you know the tower is not even open, there's a big flag in the middle of the fence, a big US flag over the fence. A big plane, you know, coming in at quarter to six in the morning, shows that you know, there's some kind of involvement.

AMY GOODMAN: How many US military left with you on the plane?

FRANZ GABRIEL: 20.

AMY GOODMAN: How many security?

FRANZ GABRIEL: About 18.

AMY GOODMAN: Are they all US?

FRANZ GABRIEL: Yes.

AMY GOODMAN: So, there were 38 with security and military?

FRANZ GABRIEL: Mm-hmm. And there's some Steele guys had their wives with them. And a baby that was probably a year old.

AMY GOODMAN: So they figured this out very fast, to get to the airplane and get their families to the airport. How did they get their families to the airport?

FRANZ GABRIEL: Well, it happened very fast because somehow—between the US Embassy, and some of the Steel guys, there was some communication.

AMY GOODMAN: So they knew before the President, that the President was being taken to the airport?

FRANZ GABRIEL: Yes. That is the only thing I can…

AMY GOODMAN: And what happened to everyone? Did they all come here?

FRANZ GABRIEL: They all came here and left.

Aristide's bodyguard Franz Gabriel speaking in the presidential palace in Bangui.

CHAPTER FIFTEEN

US Warns Aristide: Stay Out of Hemisphere

Tuesday, March 16th, 2004

Rep. Maxine Waters, Randall Robinson, lawyer Ira Kurzban, and Jamaican envoy Sharon Hay-Webster talk with Democracy Now! about the return of Aristide and the reaction from the US and Haiti.

President Aristide's arrival in Jamaica has sparked a major controversy in the Caribbean. The US-installed Prime Minister of Haiti, Gerard Latortue, has recalled Haiti's ambassador to Jamaica. He has accused Jamaican Prime Minister P. J. Patterson of committing what he called an unfriendly act. He has also announced that he is freezing Haiti's participation in CARICOM, the 15-member organization of Caribbean nations. CARICOM has called for an independent investigation into the circumstances of Aristide's removal from Haiti.

Meanwhile, senior officials of the Bush administration have expressed their opposition to Aristide being in the Western Hemisphere. James Foley, the US Ambassador to Haiti, said Jamaica was taking on a "risk and a responsibility" in welcoming Aristide. He said "His coming within 150 miles from Haiti is promoting violence."

National Security Adviser Condoleezza Rice said Sunday on NBC's "Meet the Press," "We think it's a bad idea. We believe that President Aristide, in a sense, forfeited his ability to lead his people, because he did not govern democratically."

On Sunday, before Aristide began his return back to the

Caribbean, Defense Secretary Donald Rumsfeld said on CNN "The hope is that he will not come back into the hemisphere and complicate [the] situation."

Onboard the plane yesterday, I got a chance to get reaction to the US position from the delegation that escorted Aristide to Jamaica. I talked to TransAfrica founder Randall Robinson, Rep. Maxine Waters, Jamaican Member of Parliament and CARICOM representative Sharon Hay-Webster and Aristide's lawyer, Ira Kurzban. We begin with Randall Robinson.

RANDALL ROBINSON: Condoleezza Rice, Colin Powell and Donald Rumsfeld should be ashamed of themselves. President Aristide is the democratically-elected President, the last time by 92% majority of Haiti, and he has come home to the Caribbean where he belongs. He is the President, democratically elected of the democracy that they overthrew. America ought to be ashamed of itself. And we're proud of the role we've played in bringing him home to his region where he belongs and where we hope he will stay.

AMY GOODMAN: What about the US Ambassador to Haiti, James Foley, saying that P. J. Patterson has taken a great risk and responsibility in accepting Aristide in Jamaica and, that President Aristide should not be within a 150 miles of [inaudible].

RANDALL ROBINSON: Well, Prime Minister Patterson has done a great thing. And what Mr. Foley says sounds like a threat to me. It is emblematic of the kind of arrogance with which America imposes its policy on the region and on the world. It's a disgrace. And we, as Americans, must fight against that. It is intolerable what they have done in Haiti. And what they are doing in many other parts of the world. And there is no question that this President was fairly elected twice and the last time by a huge majority. And to suggest that he is not to come back to the region, to which he belongs, is totally unacceptable.

REP. MAXINE WATERS: It is inconceivable that this administration has helped to foster a coup against Haiti and helped to oust a democratically-elected president and then have the audacity to say that he can never reside in his own region.

AMY GOODMAN: Congressmember Maxine Waters.

REP. MAXINE WATERS: His neighboring country has offered him the opportunity to be there temporarily is just the arrogance of this kind of position that is upsetting to so many Americans.

This was a democratically-elected President. He was not the cause of violence in Haiti. As a matter of fact, we begged Colin Powell and our own government to help stabilize Haiti when the so-called rebels, those people who have been a part of the death squads in Haiti previously had come into the country and were now threatening to cause violence. We asked them to help stabilize Haiti and they refused to do it. This President didn't cause any violence and there is no reason to believe that he will cause any in the future. I think it's outrageous for Condoleezza Rice or Colin Powell or Mr. Foley to be making those kinds of statements.

We have to set the record straight. Many Americans still don't know exactly what took place in Haiti. As a matter of fact, for Mr. Foley to tell a duly-elected Prime Minister of a country what he should and should not be doing is absolutely outrageous. Mr. Foley was not elected by anybody. And I think he should confine his comments to managing his own job.

AMY GOODMAN: Are you surprised by Colin Powell making these statements, given that you've been communicating with him?

REP. MAXINE WATERS: Well, certainly Colin Powell knew that Jamaica was going to receive President Aristide. He did say at one point that he would not have chosen anywhere in the Caribbean or Jamaica, but he knew that he was going to Jamaica and he assisted us in working with the government of CAR. by letting them know that the United States did not have a hold on him. So, this comes as no surprise to him. And I don't know what all of this talk is about this morning.

IRA KURZBAN: This is Ira Kurzban. The statements issued by Colin Powell and Condoleezza Rice, Ambassador Foley should be shocking to every American. A core value of our society is the right of people to travel freely and, in fact, there seems to be some obvious contradiction in terms of what they're saying because these are the same people who complain about the fact that people can't travel freely from Cuba or can't travel freely to and from other countries.

So, this is the kind of doublespeak, the kind of hypocrisy, the kind of mendacity that we have seen by this administration repeatedly.

President Aristide has a right to travel freely to any country that will invite him, and Jamaica has been gracious enough to invite him to stay temporarily. The United States has no business commenting on that, let alone trying to threaten leaders of other countries for doing so.

And what's even worse, of course, here, is that we're responsible for a coup in Haiti and it is time that the truth came out about that, and that people like Ms. Rice and Mr. Powell own up to what the United States has done. To now make it worse by trying to send the President into exile, like the French did to other leaders, shows how far we've regressed as a nation and as an administration.

Finally, and probably the worst aspect of this, is Secretary Powell keeps saying how unpopular President Aristide is. Well, what is this administration afraid of? If President Aristide is as unpopular as they say he is in Haiti, then why are they afraid of having him a hundred miles from Haiti?

Again, it's a kind of doublespeak, the kinds of lies that Powell and Rice and the others with weapons of mass destruction and everything else that they've repeated to the American people. And I think people finally needed to wake up and realize what it is they're doing. They can't, on one hand, say how unpopular President Aristide is and then say they're afraid to have him 100 miles away from Haiti because he is going to cause trouble.

It strikes at a core value of our society, which is the right for all people to travel freely. All Americans believe that. And certainly President Aristide has the right to accept an invitation wherever he is given, whether it is ten miles away from Haiti, whether it is 100 miles or whether it's in Haiti itself.

And the reality is that if they cared enough about the situation, they would make sure that there is a democratically-elected leader reinstated in his country because President Aristide won the last election by 92% of the vote. He won his first election by 67% of the vote. And the people who the United States has now appointed to run Haiti are people who have never been elected to any public office.

SHARON HAY-WEBSTER: The Prime Minister [inaudible] President of CARICOM responded to a request from President Aristide. He consulted with his colleagues who are also leaders within the region. And they agreed to host him here in Jamaica.

AMY GOODMAN: Sharon Hay-Webster, Jamaican member of Parliament.

SHARON HAY-WEBSTER: I don't know any other leader who has been ousted from the country and not been allowed to return to the country, much less as having our own family members come back to the region. I think the fact that we've heard these responses speaks to the level of success that we've had [inaudible] of this mission.

AMY GOODMAN: What about this issue of serious risk and responsibility that Prime Minister—

SHARON HAY-WEBSTER: I believe all appropriate considerations have been taken. Prime Minister Patterson has served as minister of foreign affairs. He has been Prime Minister for over ten years. He has a wealth of considerable experience and leadership and I don't believe that he has any reason to second guess this decision having been taken and this has been bolstered by the other members of CARICOM. This is not a lone or a personal decision, and I think it is an excellent one.

AMY GOODMAN: And the idea that the 150-mile radius could cause unrest in Haiti?

SHARON HAY-WEBSTER: In that case, then, it proves that Aristide has far more support than the media and those who are now speaking have been willing to give him credit for.

AMY GOODMAN: The letter that you delivered to the President of the Central African Republic, what does it say and [inaudible].

SHARON HAY-WEBSTER: It is from Prime Minister Patterson, chairman of CARICOM. It advised Mr. [inaudible] that I was his special emissary and that I had come as an emissary from CARICOM to take Mr. Aristide home to the Caribbean, and thanked him for his courtesies and asked him to extend the necessary courtesies and allow us to take him home with us, and that is what we're about to do. We're two hours away from home and we're very happy to be doing that, especially in respect with the fact that it has been a tremendous symbol that we saved. In terms of [inaudible] between the Black Diaspora in the Western Hemisphere, and Mother Africa.

AMY GOODMAN: And the feeling in Jamaica about Jean-Bertrand Aristide?

SHARON HAY-WEBSTER: There is mixed reaction. There are those who are supportive and there are those who are not. It's a democratic country.

REP. MAXINE WATERS: If Ambassador Foley is concerned about violence, or disruption, he should look right in Haiti where they have supported—

AMY GOODMAN: Congresswoman Maxine Waters.

REP. MAXINE WATERS: Supported the so-called rebels who are in Haiti. If he is concerned about violence, why did he and our government, the Bush government do nothing to stop Mr. Jodel Chamblain. Why have they done nothing to stop the people who are obviously perpetrating the violence in Haiti? And in addition, if they are worried about somebody creating some violence, why did they allow Constant who is known to have killed thousands of Haitians on the CIA payroll to reside up in New Jersey in the United States? I think this is an absolutely ridiculous statement on his part.

RANDALL ROBINSON: The United States took President Aristide against his will to the Central African Republic. Without his consent, without his knowledge, and placed him in a country that has no diplomatic relations with the community of Africa, because it came to power in a coup, has no diplomatic relations with the United States, and it is as remote from the Caribbean as any country in Africa or indeed in the world. So that he would be hard to reach there.

We brought him home, because the Caribbean is where he belongs. Twice elected democratically, the last time by a 94% majority, in an election that the United States has now overthrown, taken him far away with the idea that he would be kept there against his will.

It was clear last night, before the President agreed to release Mr. Aristide to us to take back to the Caribbean, that he would only do so after he had been cleared to do so by France and the United States. He was being held there against his will, not by the Central African Republic, but by the United States and France. It is a vivid disgrace that America would be involved in something so shoddy as this whole enterprise.

And now, to threaten Jamaica, as if to say that it is prepared to do to Jamaica what it did to Haiti is simply detestable.

CHAPTER SIXTEEN

President Aristide in His Own Words

DN!'s Exclusive Interview, Part 1

Tuesday, March 16th, 2004

Highlights from Amy Goodman's exclusive televised interview with Haitian President Aristide while he flew back to the Caribbean. Part 2 will air on Wednesday's Democracy Now!

President Aristide on Returning to the Caribbean

PRESIDENT ARISTIDE: CARICOM, on behalf of the people of the region, expressed solidarity with the Haitian people, when the coup, which I call a kidnapping, happened last February 28th, 29th. This opportunity gives me a good chance say "thank you" to the chairman of CARICOM, Prime Minister Patterson, to the heads, to all our brothers and sisters of the Caribbean family.

AMY GOODMAN: What do you think this means to the people of Haiti, your return to the Caribbean?

PRESIDENT ARISTIDE: Obviously they know how connected we are because they're suffering. It is my suffering. When they feel I will be closer, I'm convinced they'll feel better. Although they know being far doesn't mean a way to not be connected to them.

President Aristide on Whether he Resigned

PRESIDENT ARISTIDE: No, I didn't resign. What some people call "resignation" is a "new *coup d'etat*," or "modern kidnapping."

President Aristide on Why the US Wanted Him Out of Office

PRESIDENT ARISTIDE: If you ask the US the question, they would answer you. I can have opinions, but I will not answer for them. For instance, we are the first black independent country in the world. We just celebrated 200 years of independence last January 1st. Despite that, we still have 1.5 doctors for each 11,000 Haitians. And, of course, I understood we had to invest in education. We had to invest in health care. Despite an economic embargo they imposed upon us, I did my best, and we founded a university, whose faculty of medicine already had 247 medical students. Once the Marines arrived in Haiti, they put those 247 medical students out, they seized the classroom, the campus; and that's where you find soldiers, where you should have medical students. So, it's to say, if I look at the picture, which is horrible, I can think once you want to invest in education, in health care, those who want to invest in killing democracy, in bloodshed, they don't accept you as an elected president. We had 32 *coup d'etats*, plus the last one, 33, in our 200 years of independence. Our goal was to move not from *coup d'etat* to *coup d'etat* anymore, but from elections to elections. Free, fair and democratic elections. That wasn't their goal. They went back to *coup d'etat*.

President Aristide on the Haitian Coup

PRESIDENT ARISTIDE: …. they broke the constitutional order by using force to have me out of the country…

AMY GOODMAN: How did it happen?

PRESIDENT ARISTIDE: I will not go to details. Maybe next time. But as I said, they used force. When you have militaries coming from abroad surrounding your house, taking control of the airport, surrounding the national palace, being in the streets, and take you from your house to put you in the plane where you have to spend 20 hours without knowing where they were going to go with you, without talking about details which I already did somehow in other occasions. It was using force to take an elected president out of his country.

AMY GOODMAN: And was that the US military that took you out?

PRESIDENT ARISTIDE: There were US military and I suspect it could be also completed with the presence of all the militaries from other countries.

AMY GOODMAN: When they came to your house in the early morning of February 29 was it US military that came?

PRESIDENT ARISTIDE: There were diplomats, there were US military, there were US people.

AMY GOODMAN: And what did they tell you?

PRESIDENT ARISTIDE: Well, as I said, I prefer not go into details right now because I already talk about the details on other occasions. And it's also opportunities for me to help the people focusing on the results of that kidnapping. They still continue to kill Haitians in Haiti; and Haitians continue to flee Haiti by boat. People and others have to go to hiding, others courageously went to the streets to demonstrate in a peaceful way, asking for my return and when we know what happened to those they killed, we have concerns about what may happen to those who peacefully demonstrate for my return.

AMY GOODMAN: The Bush administration said that when you—after you got on the plane, when you were leaving, you spoke with CARICOM leaders. Is this true?

PRESIDENT ARISTIDE: They lied. I never had any opportunity from February 28 at night, when this started, to the minute I arrived in CAR. I never had any conversation with anyone from CARICOM within that framework of time.

AMY GOODMAN: How many US military were on the plane with you?

PRESIDENT ARISTIDE: I cannot know how many were there but I know it's the plane with 55 seats. Among them we had 19 American agents from Steele Foundation, which is a

US company providing security to the President, the First Lady, VIP people, based on an agreement which was signed between the government of Haiti and that US company called the Steele Foundation. So, they put those 19 American agents in that plane and there were five by my side. There were two Haitian ladies, wives of two American agents plus a baby one year and a half. The rest they were American militaries.

AMY GOODMAN: Were they dressed in military uniform?

PRESIDENT ARISTIDE: They were not only dressed in—with their uniform, it was like if they were going to war for the first period of time—on the ground, when we went to the plane. After the plane took off, that's the way they were. Then they changed, moving from the uniform to other kind of clothes.

AMY GOODMAN: Civilian clothes?

PRESIDENT ARISTIDE: Yes.

AMY GOODMAN: And did they go with you all the way to the Central African Republic?

PRESIDENT ARISTIDE: They did, without telling me where they were taking me, without telling me how long it would take us to be there. And the most cynical happened with that baby one year and a half old, it was when they—when the father wanted to get out with him, this is what I heard, they told him no. So, that little baby had to spend all this time sitting in a military plane, arriving in CAR, he and his father had to go back with the same plane. So, only God knows the kind of suffering he went through.

AMY GOODMAN: Did these people ever get off the plane in the Central African Republic with all the military and security—

PRESIDENT ARISTIDE: I cannot tell you because once I got out of the plane, I was well received by five members—five ministers of the government of President Joseph Bozize. So, being with them at that time, I don't know how they managed after I left.

AMY GOODMAN: Did the Steele Foundation bring in reinforcements when the situation got more dangerous?

PRESIDENT ARISTIDE: No, because Saturday night when they came to me, they told me (A) US officials ordered them to leave and to leave immediately; (B) the 25 American agents that were supposed to welcome the day after, February 29, to reinforce their team, couldn't leave the US to join them in Haiti. So that was a very strong message to them and to us.

AMY GOODMAN: Can you repeat that, what were the regulations?

PRESIDENT ARISTIDE: Please? I don't get the question?

AMY GOODMAN: Could you repeat that, what happened with the Steele foundation employees? What you just said about the reinforcements?

PRESIDENT ARISTIDE: I said that Saturday 29, 28 at night when they came to me, they told me that, (A) they ordered them to leave and immediately; (B) the day after, February 29, they were supposed to welcome another team of 25 American agents to reinforce them on the ground and US officials prevented those 25 to leave the United States to go to Haiti to join them.

AMY GOODMAN: And that's what the Steele Foundation told you?

PRESIDENT ARISTIDE: Exactly.

AMY GOODMAN: Did they say why the US said that?

PRESIDENT ARISTIDE: Well, I didn't go through the details with them. But it was obvious in my mind that was part of the global plan. The global plan was to kidnap me, *coup d'e-tat*, of course that presented one piece of the picture.

CHAPTER SEVENTEEN

Exclusive:

President Aristide in His Own Words

DN!'s Exclusive Interview, Part 2

Wednesday, March 17th, 2004

P art 2 of Democracy Now!'s exclusive broadcast of Amy Goodman's interview with Haitian President Jean-Bertrand Aristide aboard his flight from the Central African Republic to Jamaica.

Since winning independence from the French 200 years ago through a revolutionary slave revolt, Haiti has seen 33 military coups. Jean-Bertrand Aristide is the man overthrown in the two most recent ones.

In 1991, less than a year after becoming the first democratically-elected leader in Haiti's history, Aristide was overthrown by paramilitary death squads working closely with US intelligence agencies. After a few years in exile, Aristide returned to Haiti in 1994 in a US military plane to serve the remaining few months left in his term.

In 2000, Aristide won the presidential election a second time. Once again, a few years after being elected, Aristide has been overthrown in a coup—by many of same men who led the armed insurrection against him a decade earlier. People like Louis Jodel Chamblain, the former number two man in FRAPH convicted in absentia for the 1994 Raboteau massacre and the September 11, 1993 assassination of democracy-activist Antoine Izméry; Guy Philippe, a former police chief who fled Haiti in October 2000 after authorities discovered him plotting a coup with a clique of other police chiefs who had all been trained by US Special Forces in Ecuador during the 1991-1994 coup, and Jean Tatoune another leader of FRAPH, also convicted of massacre in Raboteau.

Two weeks ago after being taken by force to the Central African Republic in what Aristide calls a US-orchestrated *coup d'etat*, the Haitian President defied Washington this weekend and returned to the Caribbean. He is now in Jamaica, just 130 miles or so from Haiti.

I was one of two journalists allowed on the plane that took a delegation of US and Jamaican officials to escort President Aristide and his wife, Mildred, back to the Caribbean. As we crossed the Atlantic on our way to Kingston, Jamaica, I had a chance to conduct an extensive interview with President Aristide on-board the Gulfstream jet.

Today we play Part 2 of my interview with Aristide, where he discusses his time as president, the first coup, disbanding the military and more:

JEAN-BERTRAND ARISTIDE: We had an army of 7,000 soldiers controlling 40% of the national region. Not only they led those coup, they had 32 *coup d'etats*, the last one 33. After the coup they led in 1991, they and members of a criminal organization, well known FRAPH, killed more than 5,000 Haitians. Some people don't like to hear 5,000 because for them it could be double or more than that. Let's say more than 5,000 people were killed by the army at that time with the help of the well-known criminal organization called FRAPH. When I went back on October 15, 1994, it was obvious that the Haitian people couldn't go ahead with killers. The Haitian people wanted people to protect them, not people to kill them. So, the army was disbanded. Now they reached a way to have more drug dealers, like Guy Philippe who was arrested for drugs in Panama, sent back to Santo Domingo and then back to Haiti with the assistance of those who pretend to restore peace to Haiti, Chamblain was already convicted twice and now he is back. So having criminals, drug dealers, thugs who were convicted to come back with an army, then when they guess what we had through those 32 *coup d'etats*, leading Haiti from misery to misery while we want to move from misery to poverty with dignity, this is maybe what they have in their minds.

AMY GOODMAN: When the CARICOM-US Group came and negotiated the US-backed peace plan that you accepted with Noriega, Roger Noriega, Assistant Secretary of State representing the United States, how did they refer to the opposition, how did they refer to the people you just described as Jodel Chamblain, Guy Philippe?

JEAN-BERTRAND ARISTIDE: The meeting we had with members of my government and diplomats and heads of international delegations in my office, Mr. Noriega referring to those thugs terrorists said "I will call them killers," that's what he said. I'm shocked when today I still see members of the international community acting with those killers. More than that accompanying Guy Philippe, a killer, to distribute food to people, so trying to project another image of him when as a well-known drug dealer and a killer he should be put in jail. So, it is scandalous. The world needs to know that. The more they listen to what is going on in Haiti today, the more they may join the Haitian people to prevent the killers to continue to do the same, killing people.

AMY GOODMAN: Jean-Bertrand Aristide on board the chartered jet as we headed over the Atlantic. The US delegation headed by congressmember Maxine Waters and the Jamaican member of parliament Sharon Hay-Webster, bringing the Aristides to Jamaica, this as members of the Bush administration from Condoleezza Rice to Donald Rumsfeld warned that Jean-Bertrand Aristide should not return to this hemisphere. I asked Haitian President Jean-Bertrand Aristide if he could talk about the killing of the justice minister in Haiti in 1993; Louis Jodel Chamblain, one of the current so-called rebels, was convicted of murdering Guy Mallory. This was Jean-Bertrand Aristide's response.

JEAN-BERTRAND ARISTIDE: From 1991 to 1994, the Minister of Justice, Guy Mallory, Father Mallory's son, Antoine Izmery, the people they killed [inaudible] lost their lives because they were calling for democracy, the restoration of the constitutional order for my return to Haiti. After I returned, we had a trial. And Chamblain was convicted by a court of US. Twice. In spite of that, nothing happened, only impunity and assistance and heavy machine guns were provided to him and the orders to have them appearing as rebels, as if they were not anymore killers, people already convicted. This is the cynical picture.

AMY GOODMAN: We have our September 11, 2001. Chile has their September 11, 1973, the day that Salvador Allende died in the palace as the Pinochet forces rose to power. You have two separate September 11ths, 1988 and 1993. Can you describe what happened to you and your parish, your congregation on September 11, 1988 at San Jean Bosco?

JEAN-BERTRAND ARISTIDE: We were praying, we were celebrating our faith in god, and for us god means love, peace, justice, freedom, solidarity. Getting together to pray means empowering all those who share the same faith. If you stand up for justice, then you cannot close the eyes to not see poor people willing to have jobs, to eat with dignity. Once you stand up for that, then you may have people not only rejecting you but also putting fire in a church, burning people. This is what happened that day, September 11, 1988. When we had it elsewhere, not in a church but in a country like Chile and President Allende willing to stand up for human beings, for the right to eat, the right to go to school, the right to have health care, and so and so, people who don't care about human beings rejected that *coup d'etat.* When on September 11th 2001, something tragic happened in the United States called terrorism, we saw the world rejecting terrorism. Asked if when, for instance, we have Guy Philippe, Chamblain, well known as terrorists, drug dealers, convicted people, armed by those who pretend helping Haiti to kill Haitians, it's like if...it's not anymore terrorism. So, racism, somehow is linked to that cynical game.

AMY GOODMAN: This is Democracy Now! "The War and Peace Report." I'm Amy Goodman. As we continue with the interview with President Aristide, I had asked the Haitian President on board this flight where he and his wife traveled for 17 hours to get back to Jamaica, you can go to our website at democracynow.org to see the chronicle of this trip: brought to the Central African Republic by the United States with dozens of US military and security, taken there, the early hours of February 29, taken out of Haiti, not knowing where they were going. They said told by the—one of top men in the US Embassy, Louis Moreno, who had come to the President's residence, that he would be going to address the press. Instead, he was rushed on to a—he was rushed on to a US plane. I asked Jean-Bertrand Aristide if he could go back in time, as we look at the current rebel leaders like Chamblain, convicted of the murders of not only the justice minister in 1993, Guy Mallory, but the Haitian businessman, Antoine Izmery, in 1993 about this significance of Haiti's September 11 in 1988, the massacre at the church, Jean-Bertrand Aristide's church. He had been a priest. And that happened September 11, 1988. Five years later, September 11, 1993, the Haitian multimillionaire businessman Antoine Izmery joined a procession to remember the victims of the massacre and he, too, was executed. I asked Jean-Bertrand Aristide about this.

JEAN-BERTRAND ARISTIDE: On September 11, 1988, they burned the church, they burned people, killed people as I explained. While I was in exile, Antoine Izmery went to the church of Sacre Coeur on the same day, on September 11, to remember what happened in 1988, to bring his solidarity to the parents, relatives, friends of the victims and also to empower those who are peacefully fighting for our return, which was clearly the restoration of democracy to Haiti. And the same people who made it happen in Saint-Jean Bosco made it happen again in Sacre Coeur. The worst was already bad, but it's shameful when we see today, the same hands, killing people, burning houses almost the same way.

AMY GOODMAN: Jodel Chamblain was convicted of Izmery's murder?

JEAN-BERTRAND ARISTIDE: Yes. Yes.

AMY GOODMAN: Yet when we watch television, where most people get their news and information, we almost never hear them mentioned.

JEAN-BERTRAND ARISTIDE: We will not, since last November, they brought to Haiti a good number of journalists. We fought hard for the freedom of press. So we will continue to respect the rights of every single journalist. But unfortunately, what happened from November to today is a tragic event where it seems money was spent to bribe journalists, not all of them, but some of them, money was used to finance radio stations playing the card of so-called opposition, linked to Chamblain, linked to Guy Philippe, being their voices. When Jean Tautoune was convicted, put in jail, escaped from jail, and giving interviews to those radio stations, to TVs, which kind of impunity are we talking about? Which kind of freedom for the press are we talking about? Is it freedom for the press as a cover for impunity? Or as a full place where you use your rights to talk, to criticize, to say what you want? Yes. We had that in Haiti where journalists could talk. But all the journalists who were in Haiti from November to the coup or kidnapping were not there just to tell the truth. But also some of them were there because they were paid to relay the lies which sprayed this [mis]information around the world, paving the way for the kidnapping.

AMY GOODMAN: Who paid them?

JEAN-BERTRAND ARISTIDE: Every year, for the past couple of years, US $56 million went to Haiti to finance political parties—radio stations, TV stations, journalists, who got all visa from embassies, lying to discredit our fragile democracy, our money from those US $56 million. Recently, for the past year, it became US $70 million. So, this is well known. It is not a secret.

AMY GOODMAN: So, you're saying the US government forces poured this money in.

JEAN-BERTRAND ARISTIDE: That money came from abroad: US, Europe, through EU, and organizations like that.

AMY GOODMAN: Do you see similarities—

JEAN-BERTRAND ARISTIDE: And maybe this is the last question for TV.

AMY GOODMAN: OK. Do you see similarities with what happened with you and what is continuing to happen with Hugo Chavez in Venezuela?

JEAN-BERTRAND ARISTIDE: They say that IRI was behind a coup which happened in Venezuela and still behind what is going on in Venezuela.

AMY GOODMAN: The International Republican Institute?

JEAN-BERTRAND ARISTIDE: Correct. They say they have their hands through what is happening in Haiti. Often, they organize seminars for the so-called opposition where they had Guy Philippe, Chamblain and members of the Haitian opposition, training them to kill, to talk after killing, to project an image of democratic opposition with heavy machine guns on your shoulders, blood on their hands, etcetera. So, this is, from my point of view, the same hands behind the same things happening in two different countries.

AMY GOODMAN: You have information that people who support you are people who were part of Lavalas are being threatened or killed in Haiti right now?

JEAN-BERTRAND ARISTIDE: A good number of

them are in hiding. Not because they are cowards, but because this is a strategy to spend time where they may not kill you, to come back in a peaceful way and continue to support democracy calling for the restoration of the constitution of order. Others were killed. I'm very sad when they say about those who were killed. Others left the country by boat to go to Florida. And, unfortunately, when the house is on fire, those who put fire in the house are the same who send back the victims fleeing the fire put in that house. Violation of international law and attraction to have more people because as long as you continue to kill people in the country, you invite them to come to your country because they will continue to flee that occupation.

AMY GOODMAN: When you were ousted in 1991, for the three-year period, there was not only a mass movement in Haiti, but a mass movement in the United States of support and solidarity. Do you have any message you want to send to the American people?

JEAN-BERTRAND ARISTIDE: I will say thank you to all the American people who supported democracy with the Haitian people and who continue to support the Haitian people supporting democracy in Haiti. We want elections in Haiti. Free, fair, democratic elections. That means one human being, one vote, which is a democratic principle. We want to respect that principle. I know how the American people care for that democratic principle. They want to see their vote respected. As we in Haiti want to see the vote of the people respected. By supporting us, the American people support what they want to be supported in their own country and because any democratic process, which is well protected, may be good for any country where they want democratic systems. I think somehow Haiti and the United States, we are linked by democracy and democratic principles. As we are linked to all the countries where they care for that democratic principle, one human being, one vote, that's why I thank by expressing our gratitude to our friends living in the US or being US citizens. We think they find energy to continue to build solidarity with the Haitian people. Once we have Haitians in Savannah, I having—having solidarity with the American people to free the American people. Once we got our independence in Haiti, at that time Guyana by itself represented almost half of the territory of the United States at that time. So, we have in common many things. Historic ties. Principles, democratic principles, which makes it good for us to continue to work hard for democracies, which has to flourish not only in one country or in two countries, but in our region.

AMY GOODMAN: Very last question. You are going to Jamaica now, which is very close to Haiti. Do you see yourself returning to Haiti?

JEAN-BERTRAND ARISTIDE: I always paid attention to the voice of the Haitian people, as I will continue to pay attention to their voice. Paying attention to their voice respectfully I will know what to do. Thank you.

AMY GOODMAN: President Aristide, thank you very much.

* * *

At the time this book went to press in July 2004, President Aristide and his family were living in South Africa.